W!

MORE FOUL DEEDS & SUSPICIOUS DEATHS IN BIRMINGHAM

By the same author:

Foul Deeds & Suspicious Deaths in Birmingham
ISBN: 1-903425-96-4

Foul Deeds & Suspicious Deaths in Stratford & South Warwickshire
ISBN: 1-903425-99-9

More Foul Deeds & Suspicious Deaths in
BIRMINGHAM

NICK BILLINGHAM

Series Editor
Brian Elliott

Wharncliffe Books

Dedication

This book is dedicated to the officers of Birmingham Borough Police
Force who had the unenviable task of sorting these incidents out.

First Published in Great Britain in 2007 by
Wharncliffe Books
an imprint of
Pen and Sword Books Ltd
47 Church Street
Barnsley
South Yorkshire
S70 2AS

ISBN: 978-184563-026-3

A CIP catalogue record for this book is available from the
British Library.

Typeset in 10/12pt Plantin by Concept, Huddersfield.

Printed and bound in England by Biddles.

Pen and Sword Books Ltd incorporates the imprints of
Pen & Sword Aviation, Pen & Sword Maritime,
Pen & Sword Military, Wharncliffe Books,
Pen & Sword Select, Pen and Sword Military Classics
and Leo Cooper.

For a complete list of Pen & Sword titles please contact
PEN & SWORD BOOKS LIMITED
47 Church Street
Barnsley
South Yorkshire
S70 2BR
England
E-mail: enquiries@pen-and-sword.co.uk
Website: www.pen-and-sword.co.uk

Contents

Introduction

The town of Birmingham stretches a long way back into the mists of time. It traces its roots back to an age where farming was the only activity of any consequence. However, this is not a book of history but of the stories within history; what people got up to. The most dramatic of these were recorded in newspapers and journals, folk memories and the landscape itself. By the eighteenth century, Birmingham was well on the way to becoming a major conurbation, home to engineers and inventors, skilled metal workers and thousands of trades allied to them. Unlike the industrial towns in the North that relied on a single industry – like cotton – Birmingham maintained a broad range of trades and was thus spared those awful 'dark satanic mills' so typical of the Industrial Revolution.

Murders in the eighteenth century were very rare, although you could be hanged for stealing a sheep or being involved in a riot. Unfortunately, few of these incidents were well recorded and it is not until the nineteenth century that crime reporting became as detailed as a researcher might like. Throughout the nineteenth and into the twentieth century, newspaper reporters brought all the grisly details of a murder to their readers in well-crafted journalism. Sad to say, the introduction of photographs saw a decline in the detail reported. By the Second World War, journalism had shrunk to a few photographs and some salacious headlines. For the most part this unhappy state of affairs has persisted to the present day.

Violence in the eighteenth century was rife, so much so that few ordinary affrays made it into the papers, but every now and then the city exploded into riot. During the 1790s there were several riots caused by the price of food. It was a world still totally dependent on agriculture and a series of bad harvests spelt catastrophe. The price of wheat went up, followed by the price of other grains, until bread was a luxury that few workers could afford. On 29 June 1795, Mr Pickard's corn mill and bakery became the focus of a riot, sparked off when he reduced

A view of Birmingham in the late eighteenth century. R K Dent

the size of a loaf. Rumours soon swirled round the town that he had secretly buried a hoard of wheat under the mill. A mob of hungry women descended on the mill and started to ransack it. A couple of magistrates then tried to read the Riot Act but had stones thrown at them. The Dragoons and Cavalry were called in and a pitched battle ensued. At one point one of the Dragoons fired indiscriminately into the seething crowd. The bullet passed clean through the chest of a young man called Allen, killing him instantly, and then buried itself into Henry Mason, mortally wounding him. The mob dispersed and two women and a man were arrested as ring leaders. Margaret Bowlker, Mary Mullens and George Hattory were sent to Warwick Gaol to await trial. In the August assizes Margaret was sentenced to death and hanged outside Warwick Gaol. This was just one of many riots caused by the succession of poor harvests at the end of the eighteenth century. An apparently ruthless judiciary maintained the social order of the day, but we

COUNCIL HOUSE, BIRMINGHAM.

The riches generated by the thousands of trades enabled the Victorians to rebuild the city with real civic pride. Author's collection

must not forget that the mob actions were driven by a fear of starvation and utter poverty.

In old fashioned days Birmingham Prison was something of a joke. In medieval times offenders were kept in a dungeon of the manor house, but in 1733 a 'proper' prison was built in Peck

Lane. It had a couple of dank cells in the cellar and during the riots of 1775 these had to hold 150 people. They were about 8 feet by 5 feet, although during that riot it was standing room only, even upstairs in the gaoler's rooms. Things weren't quite as organised as today. The gaoler was not paid a salary and so had to earn his money from the prisoners, mostly by brewing beer and selling it to them. The prisoners were only given two chunks of bread and cheese each day, so they bought what they could. Once all their money was gone, the gaoler needed some other customers, so the prison became a part-time pub, punters and prisoners drinking together. The gaoler had to be on his toes to make sure the right people left at closing time. Nothing remains of this rather casual prison now, it lies somewhere underneath New Street Station.

The nineteenth century dawned to a new era of steam engines and coach travel. The town had no official police force but the High Bailiff and magistrates hired constables and watchmen to keep order. On the night of 18 July 1805, one of the constables, Robert Twiford, was patrolling the streets around Snow Hill when a suspicious character he had stopped to question, shot him. Robert took a fair while to die of his injuries, and he managed to give a good description of the villain. Philip Matsell was duly arrested and hauled off to Warwick for trial.

One peculiarity of the era was that murderers were often executed and gibbeted at the scene of the crime. Although Margaret Bowlker had been hung outside Warwick Gaol, Philip Matsell was sentenced to be hung at the site of the shooting, Snow Hill. It created one of the strangest spectacles the town can have ever seen. No one had been executed in Birmingham before. A gibbet and scaffold were built at the bottom of Great Charles Street and on 22 August Matsell was brought in a covered cart from Warwick. At Camp Hill, thousands of people waited to see the condemned man as he was pinioned by the arms and placed in an open cart alongside the hangman and a clergyman. The procession wound its way through Deritend to the scaffold. The scene was astounding, virtually the entire population of the town, 50,000, had turned up, some jeering, some sobbing, others selling trinkets. The throng was so dense that the clergy and guards could barely keep hold of Matsell, let alone even start to read the prayers for the condemned man. It was chaos.

The only person who managed to retain his dignity was Matsell himself. He told the clergyman exactly where he could put his bible and climbed up the ladder to the scaffold on his own. Without waiting for the hangman to catch up, he managed to put on the noose. Matsell shouted: 'Here Goes!' and jumped.

For several weeks, his body swung 20 feet above the busy street as a dire warning to anyone minded to shoot a constable.

Not long after Matsell was executed, the city fathers replaced the old Peck Lane gaol with a new modern affair in Moor Street. It was combined with various civic offices and was substantially more secure. All this palaver of getting prisoners to and from Warwick came to an end in 1839 when the town of Birmingham was big enough to justify holding the Quarter Sessions there instead of at Warwick. That same year, a modern police force was founded, although for the first three years it was administered from London; and when the town obtained its charter in 1842 it became a proper locally accountable force. It was in 1849 that Winson Green Prison opened. The old gaol was built for an era when the town was much smaller. Winson Green soon earned itself a fearsome reputation for the harshness of its regime. Within four years no less than seventeen prisoners had committed suicide, victims of a system of brutal discipline. The first few governors were real martinets, with a taste for quite sadistic discipline and it took a public inquiry to get the place running on a vaguely humane regime. The place became the last home for many of the characters you will meet in this book.

The social reforms of the mid-nineteenth century brought about the establishment of not only a new prison at Winson Green. A handful of constables were also replaced by a well-disciplined force of several hundred men. The city fathers no longer had to rely on calling out the army when things got a tad riotous, which is just as well since the food riots of the eighteenth century were replaced by a few, but spectacular, sectarian riots in the nineteenth century.

Although the mid-nineteenth century saw the building of a new gaol with a stark regime, it also brought the construction of new hospitals and a more enlightened treatment of the sick, poor and elderly. This new sensibility was not reflected in the behaviour of the people. Our society might have been evolving, but the same old vices just carried on as usual. Lust, jealousy, revenge and anger kept the justices and newspapers as busy as ever they did in earlier times. Throughout this book are instances of every deadly sin and if these aren't enough there are plenty of cases of undiagnosed insanity; and also some latent tendency to violence erupting out of seemingly placid relationships. In this book, if you find a character that loves his wife to bits, you can be sure that they are several bits, hastily concealed!

The problem for the judges was that most of these cases were far from black and white arguments. In many cases the reason for a murder appears to have been completely absent, the murderer still protesting that he passionately loved the woman he had just shot and he couldn't remember anything about it. Such cases, with their undertones of some latent insanity, posed the question that if a man was mentally ill, was he responsible for his actions? Mental illness was only just being recognised, let alone understood. A century earlier, there would have been suspicions of demonic possession or witchcraft. The Victorian world was becoming more rational, but it was a difficult process.

One aspect of murder and punishment that has appeared through the 150 years that this book covers is the public attitude to capital punishment. As the nineteenth century opened you could be hanged for an assortment of quite trivial offences. In 1808 William Booth was found not guilty of murdering his brother, despite some fairly damning evidence. He was later found guilty of forging coins at his farm in Perry Barr, and was sent to the gallows for it. His execution went down in folk history. The magistrates at Stafford had built a brand new scaffold, and Booth was the first to try it out. The hangman was so concerned to put on a good show for the several thousand spectators that he forgot to tie the other end of the rope down. He dropped the trapdoor and Booth plummeted all the way to the ground, the rope following him down. At the second go, the trapdoor wouldn't open at all and he was more or less getting a slow handclap by the third attempt. This time it worked, much to Booth's annoyance.

The option of transportation was a much used alternative to capital punishment. As the nineteenth century wore on its use diminished, partly because we were running out of places to send people. Public executions tended to be fairly riotous affairs, and were becoming increasingly abhorrent to the gentry with their refined sensibilities. Parliament insisted that executions took place inside the prisons after 1868. This may have reduced the chances of civil disorder, but protests against the ultimate punishment gradually increased through the nineteenth century. The protest movement continued and the number of hangings gradually reduced. The alternative of life imprisonment meant more and larger gaols had to be built. The arguments against capital punishment finally won the day after the Second World War. The death penalty did not seem to be a deterrent during its period of use. Obviously it stopped re-offending pretty thoroughly, but it had no effect at all in deterring those completely unhinged maniacs who let rip with guns and knives for no readily understandable reason.

Despite everything, you don't really need to lock yourself away in a fortress to keep out the hordes of murderous psychopaths. Birmingham is a big place and, considering the number of people here, the number of murders is tiny. By far the largest proportion of them are domestic affairs. The chances of being killed by a stranger are miniscule; the person you really have to worry about is the one you married!

Old factories were constantly demolished to make way for new trades and businesses.
Author's collection

Acknowledgements

Many thanks are due to the staff at Birmingham Central Library Local Studies Department, Warwickshire County Records Office and the Shakespeare Birthplace Trust Records Office, without whose patient assistance this book could not have been written. Thanks are also due to the staff of Arbour Antiques, Sheep Street, Stratford-upon-Avon, for the advice and permission to photograph the antique guns featured herein.

CHAPTER 1

The Tragic End of Mary Ashford
1817

Her clothes were covered in mud, and old oak leaves covered her face.

ife in the district of Birmingham a couple of centuries ago may seem very different to our modern world, but in some respects it wasn't that different at all. Then, as now, there were parties, young lovers and, unfortunately, maniacs. The sudden death of Mary Ashford in 1817 has become one of the most famous in Birmingham's history, but possibly for the wrong reasons. The evidence surrounding her death showed fairly clearly who was responsible, but the legal system of the day was labyrinthine in its complexity and this enabled the culprit to walk from court a free man on two occasions. In the few detailed accounts, the story seems to be all about the legal side of the affair, but the evidence presented brings life around Erdington in 1817 into sharp focus. This was a world before the emergence of a city, it was a landscape of fields, where people earnt their living from the land; and yet even then there were the manufactories where metal was forged and drawn, but they were set amongst hedges and trees. The central story, however, remains the horrific fate of an attractive young woman.

Mary Ashford was just twenty in 1817. She was the very pretty daughter of a gardener who lived in a small cottage by the *Cross Keys* in Erdington. She was a vivacious girl who had a sweet nature and was considered by all who knew her to be a very virtuous and honest character. She was about 5 feet 4 inches tall. A couple of years before, she moved away from her father's overcrowded home to her uncle's farm at Langley

ABRAHAM THORNTON.   MARY ASHFORD.

A contemporary portrait of the ill-fated Mary Ashford and her alleged assailant. R K
Dent

Heath. Here, at Mr Coleman's, she was part of the household
and regularly went to market in Birmingham to sell the fruit and
vegetables from the farm.

On Whit Monday, 26 May 1817, Mary set off from the farm
to go to the market. On her way she called to see her best friend,
Hannah Cox. Hannah was working for Mr Machin in the tiny
hamlet of Erdington at the time. Mary left a bundle of evening
clothes with Hannah whilst she went off shopping. The two
talked about the dance they wanted to go to that evening. It
was the culmination of one of the Friendly Society's annual
meetings and was to be held at Tyburn House near Castle
Bromwich. Everyone who was anyone would be there. Mary
went off to the market and came back to Hannah's home at
about 6.00 pm. The two of them changed into their best
clothes. Mary had worn a pink cotton frock and scarlet spencer
(a high waisted and low neckline jacket) together with a straw
bonnet and black stockings and half boots during the day; now
she put on a clean frock, white spencer and white stockings.
Hannah had collected a new pair of shoes for Mary, especially
for the dance.

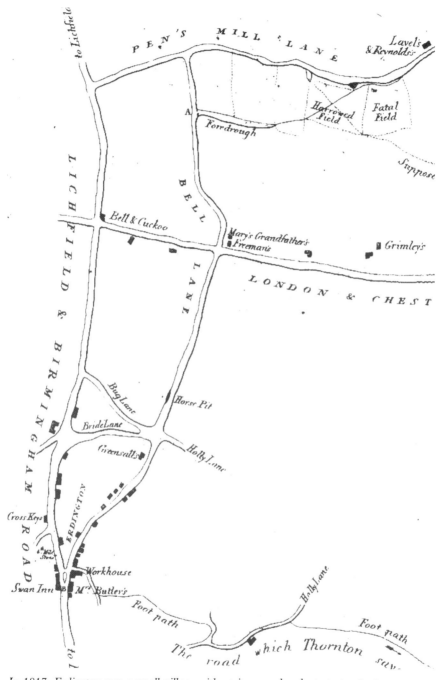

In 1817, Erdington was a small village without its own church. Author's collection

The two of them set off from Hannah's mother's house at about 7.00 pm and got to Daniel Clarke's public house, *The Three Tuns*, at about 8.30 pm. Both girls went into the dance hall in Tyburn House for a twirl, but Hannah had enough after about fifteen minutes and went into the bar to be with Benjamin Carter instead, leaving Mary dancing with Abraham Thornton.

Abraham was a supremely fit young man, considered by many to be the fittest and strongest man in the county. He was immensely stocky, with a thick-set neck and muscles bulging almost to the point of deformity. He was 5 feet 7 inches tall and appeared quite menacing because of his bulk. His face was very fat, and shining with sweat most of the time but he was agile and athletic. His father was a bricklayer and Abraham had been brought up in the family business. Bricklaying in the early 1800s was a lucrative profession; the huge number of canals being built meant they could virtually name their own price. Abraham was twenty-nine years old and a very eligible bachelor but he had a reputation for being something of a lothario.

Not long after Mary arrived, Abraham stopped dancing with the landlord's daughter and went up to Mr Cottrell to ask who the beautiful girl was. In his reply he said that she was 'old Ashford's' daughter.

Abraham replied: 'I know a sister of hers and have been connected with her three times, and I'll will with her, or I'll die by it.'

John Cooke, standing close by, was shocked at the bluntness of the statement, but he wasn't going to remonstrate with Thornton, not at the risk of getting his neck broken. Thornton went into the hall and asked Mary to dance. She accepted and they danced on through the evening. Hannah stayed in the bar with her boyfriend.

By about 11.30 pm, Hannah was ready to go home. She popped into the dance and told Mary she would be waiting outside by the canal bridge. Benjamin Carter came out and kept her company for fifteen minutes. Hannah was getting impatient and got Benjamin to go in and hurry Mary up. Eventually, Mary and Abraham came out and the four of them walked towards Erdington along the London & Chester Turnpike road. Hannah realised she had forgotten her bracelet and Benjamin ran back to the pub to get it for her, getting back to Hannah

Another contemporary portrait of Mary Ashford. She is buried in Holy Trinity Church, Sutton Coldfield. Author's collection

after about ten minutes. Benjamin walked along with Hannah for a while, but he had to get back home and left her to catch up with Mary and Abraham. This she did by the time the couple had walked as far as the junction of the lane that ran south-west towards Erdington (Grange Road is part of this old foot track today). It was at this junction that Hannah had to say goodbye, and she hurried back to her mother's house and went to bed.

Mary and Abraham walked on alone in the warm May night. The only account of what happened next is that of Abraham. Apparently, they walked on down the Chester Road to the junction with Bell Lane (now Orphanage Road). Here were two cottages, one home to Mary's grandfather and the other the Freeman family. The young couple turned right and walked down to a footpath running out into the fields. This path (Holifast Road) took them across four or five fields. They spent quite some time in these fields before walking back the way they had come. At the stile on Bell Lane they sat talking. A man with a brown jacket walked along the lane and bid them a polite 'good morning'. Abraham thought it was about 3.00 am by then. In the dim pre-dawn light it was difficult to see who it was.

Abraham asked Mary who the man was, and she said she wasn't sure but thought she had seen him at the dance. She had hidden her face from him to avoid any gossip about what they had been up to. In fact it was a man called John Umpage and he had been in a house just the other side of the road from where they had been in the fields. He had heard them talking from a little after 2.00 until 2.45. He had left the house in Penn Lane at about that time and their paths crossed by the stile on the edge of Bell Lane. John Umpage had clearly recognised Abraham Thornton, but not Mary. John had heard nothing that raised his suspicions, no raised voices, protests or suchlike, during the whole hour that they were within his earshot. He may not have been paying much attention to what they were saying because he was in deep conversation with the young lady of the house, Miss Reynolds.

The night was wearing thin and, according to Abraham, the pair of them walked back down Bell Lane towards Erdington as far as its junction with Holly Lane. Here, Abraham bid Mary good night, leaving her to walk the last few hundred yards to Hannah Cox's house alone. He said that he then waited a short while and walked down to Erdington Workhouse to see if he could see Mary again, but then decided that it was high time he went home to Castle Bromwich.

Mary walked briskly to Hannah's house. She was still wearing her dance clothes and wanted to get changed before returning home. Thomas Asprey saw her walking very fast towards the house at about 3.30 am. At about 4.00 am, Mary woke up Hannah and went into her room. Hannah noticed that her mother's clock stated it was 4.40 am. The two of them chatted away whilst Mary changed into her ordinary day clothes and wrapped up her dancing gown and white spencer around her black boots into a bundle that would be easy to carry. The sugar and other oddments she had bought at Birmingham market the day before also went into the bundle. Hannah noticed nothing unusual about Mary; she was as calm and cheerful as usual. Mary told Hannah that she had spent the night at her grandfather's house. Perhaps Hannah was a little suspicious of what had really been going on because she asked Mary how long Abraham had stayed with her and got the coy reply: 'A good bit.'

The costumes of the day were not conducive to running. R K Dent

Mary did up her straw bonnet and left Hannah at about 5.00 am, according to the clock in the house. In fact the clock was at least forty minutes fast; Hannah's mother kept it fast so she wouldn't be late for any appointments. Mary was in a contented mood and despite the long night of dancing, set off on the road back towards her grandfather's at a good pace. John Kesterton had just harnessed up his horses and was driving down Bell Lane towards Birmingham when he saw Mary come out of Hannah's mother's house and set off at a fast walk towards her grandfather's. He cracked the whip and she turned and looked at him. He reckoned it was 4.15 am. At much the same time, but a little further up Bell Lane, Mary passed Joseph Dawson. They both said: 'How do you do?', and on she walked, very fast, towards her grandfather's house.

The casual exchange with Joseph Dawson was the last time anyone but her murderer saw her alive.

George Jackson set off to work from the top of Moor Street at 5.00 am. It was a long walk, through Erdington, up Bell Lane and along the footpath that Mary and Abraham walked some hours before. The path led diagonally across a field and on to a stile into Penn's Mill Lane. Close by the stile was a water-filled pit and on the edge of this George noticed a bundle of clothes, a straw bonnet and a pair of bloodstained shoes. Realising something was very wrong, he hurried along the road until he came to Mr Lavell's cottage next door to the Reynold's. Mr Lavell was just coming out of his front door and George insisted that he come straight to the pit and stand guard over the sinister find whilst he went and raised the alarm at Penn's Mills, a factory a bit further up the road.

William Lavell waited until his work mates arrived from the mill, and then scouted around the field to see what else he could

A view of Penns Lane as it appeared in 1817. R K Dent

find. As the field had been freshly harrowed, footsteps showed clearly in the tilled soil as well as in the dew that had fallen on the grass. It was now about 6.30 am and the dew would only be visible for another hour or so. William discovered deep prints of a man's feet leading to the pit and he tracked them back to a tree. Here were the marks of where there had been a struggle. Not only was there the clear impression in the soil of a woman's body but, more ominously, two pools of blood. He looked more carefully and realised that there was a trail of blood drops in the grass about a foot to the side of the footprints. Worse still, the drops seemed to start off heavy and frequent, but gradually petered out the closer he got to the pit. Back at the pit, there was a very deep single footprint right on the edge, as though someone had sought purchase to heave something heavy into the deep dark water. James Simmons, from the mill, raced home to get a rake and some long reins to drag the pond.

William continued his painstaking search. He could now easily recognise the man's footprints. The shoes were nailed with a special type of nail called a 'Sparrow', and the pattern of these was broken on the right shoe. There was a second trail of these distinct footprints running off across the field in the direction of Castle Bromwich. He followed them until they joined the main road. Back in the harrowed field, he could make out two sets of foot prints that appeared to show a desperate chase as a man pursued a woman, gradually catching up with her, how she dodged about as he got close, sprinted away, dodged again, ran some more and ended at the tree, her silhouette preserved in the grass, arms and legs extended out. William had the good sense to fetch some planks and preserve some of the footprints from any damage.

James Simmons got back to the scene at 7.00 am with his rake. It took several attempts but eventually they managed to drag out the body of Mary Ashford. Her clothes were covered with mud, and old oak leaves clung to her face. Her sad and bedraggled corpse was carried along the road to Mr Lavell's house and laid out. Mr Joseph Webster, the owner of Penn Mills, arrived there at 8.00 am. He had arrived in his night clothes such was the panic. He was the only one around with a

A map was drawn up to show the route of Mary and her attacker across the freshly harrowed fields. Author's collection

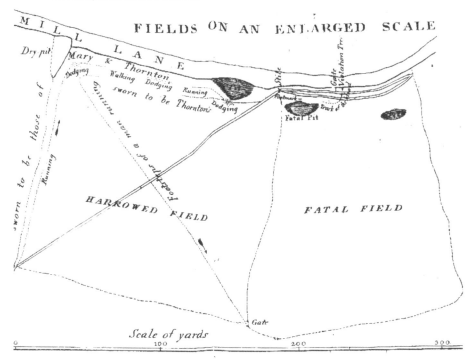

Mary Ashford was dragged from this pit a few hours after being thrown into it by her attacker. Author's collection

watch. He checked the footprints with William Lavell and found that the woman's shoes found at the edge of the pit matched the prints in the field. Back at Lavell's house, Fanny Lavell had taken the spencer off Mary's body, revealing huge bruises on each of her arms. Mr Webster went home to get dressed while Fanny struggled to get the bloodstained and ripped clothes off the body.

By 10.30 am, the news was all about the district. Mary Smith, the local nurse, examined the corpse and confirmed that Mary had been brutally raped before being thrown into the pit. The bruises on her arms appeared to be those of hands. Other bruises and lacerations covered her body. Mary Smith arranged to get the body taken to Penn Mill for a surgeon to conduct a more detailed autopsy.

The news reached Daniel Clarke at Tyburn House very early. He immediately suspected Abraham Thornton and went out to look for him. He caught up with him on the turnpike road in

Castle Bromwich, just by the chapel and said: 'What is become of the young woman that went away with you from my house last night?'

Thornton said nothing.

'She is murdered and thrown into a pit,' shouted Clarke.

'Murdered?' said Thornton.

'Yes, murdered,' confirmed Clarke.

'I [Thornton] was with her until 4 o'clock this morning.'

'Then you must go along with me and clear yourself,' said Clarke, in reply.

Thornton said he would do that, and the two of them rode back to Tyburn House. Neither of them mentioned the murder at all during the journey, just general chat about farming. Back at Tyburn House, the ponies were stabled and Thornton went inside to get something to eat and drink. He talked about walking over to Sutton in a while, but Thomas Dale had other ideas.

Constable Thomas Dale was the 'thief-taker' of Birmingham. This was long before the creation of the police force we have today. The magistrates had sent him on in advance to arrest Abraham. He found Daniel and some other men keeping him in the pub. Thomas Dale took him to an upstairs room, and William Benson and Mr Sadler joined him in searching Abraham. His shirt and underclothes were covered in dirt and bloodstained. When Thomas Dale asked how they had got into such as mess Abraham told him that he had made love to Mary – with her consent – that night. Mr Bedford, the magistrate, arrived at 11.00 am. Abraham Thornton was officially arrested for the rape and murder of Mary Ashford.

Doctor Freer arrived at Penn Mill so late in the day that there wasn't enough light for him to conduct his examination. Mary's body was moved to Tyburn House and the examination took place the next day. The magistrates and Mary's family then heard not only the ghastly facts that had already been uncovered; but yet more horror, Mary was not dead when she was thrown into the pond. She had drowned. More damning for Thornton was that his shoes were an exact match with the footprints in the field and there was blood on his clothes. He was sent to Warwick Gaol to await trial at the next assizes.

It looked like an open and shut case. On 8 August Warwick courthouse was packed to capacity as thousands travelled to see this wicked man condemned to death, and hopefully hanged. It was not to be, Abraham Thornton could afford a good counsel and pleaded not guilty on the grounds that he couldn't have been at the pit when the crime was committed because he had many and reliable witnesses to prove he was on his way back to Castle Bromwich. William and Martha Jennings were at Holden's Farm to get milk for sale in Birmingham. They were sure that they saw Abraham at 4.30 am, and they knew it was 4.30 since they had asked Jane Heaton who worked at the farm what the time was a bit earlier, and had milked a couple of cows by the time they saw Abraham walking casually down the road from the direction of Erdington. The defence then brought several other witnesses to confirm that Abraham Thornton had been closer and closer to Castle Bromwich as the morning wore on. This defence exploited the fact that there were virtually no reliable clocks in the countryside. It was common practice to note the time from the clock on St Martin's church; that was Birmingham time. The only way to set your clock at home was to first set a watch at St Martin's and then use that as a reference when you got home. Hardly anyone except the wealthy farmers and mill owners owned a watch, so it was just about impossible for most people to have any idea of the exact time. Just to make matters even more complicated, 'Birmingham time', as used in Erdington, was fifteen minutes behind of 'country time', as used in Castle Bromwich. Mr Webster made it his business to check all the times quoted by the various witnesses, by comparing their clocks to his reasonably accurate watch. He did not find any two that said the same time. Mrs Butler, Hannah's mother, had the most inaccurate clock, but they were all inaccurate to some degree. Mr Reader, Counsel for the Defence, used this ambiguity to wear down the prosecution case, but entirely omitted the possible errors when it came to the defence.

It may have been a pretty desperate defence against the evidence of bloodstained clothes and footprints, but it was just enough to plant a strong element of doubt in the minds of the jury. Justice Holroyd pointed out to them that it was vital to English justice that no innocent man should ever be sent to the gallows, that twenty guilty men going free was preferable to an innocent hanging. With his stern warning about being certain of their verdict, it took them only a few minutes to reach their decision, they didn't even retire to consider it. It was not guilty ... There was an uproar.

The charge of rape that would have followed the murder case was dropped and Abraham walked from the court a free, and very smug, man. He returned to his father's farm at Castle Bromwich.

He wasn't to remain free for long. Mary's brother, William, raised a public subscription to fund a private prosecution against him. There were several elements of the original evidence that required a further trial. The clocks were one, country time in 1817 was fifteen minutes ahead of Birmingham time, the clocks themselves were notoriously inaccurate. More sinister still was that Thomas Dale had been dismissed for improper conduct and there was a rumour going round that he had kept Thornton's handkerchief after the initial search, and that handkerchief was covered in blood. Thornton himself had allegedly admitted the rape to his fellow prisoner Homer Hall whilst he was in Warwick Gaol. Homer was prepared to give evidence to this effect if he was pardoned from his sentence of transportation. Homer's evidence was of a deeply dubious validity and was not pursued. On top of all this was the composition of the original jury; at least three and possibly four of them were all wealthy farmers known to the Thornton family, therefore open to bribery.

William Ashford used an ancient law called Appeal of Murder. This dated back to Norman times and had been used only very rarely, but usually with some success. Abraham was re-arrested and placed in Marshalsea Prison. In November, he was taken to Westminster to be tried again. Abraham finally stood in front of the Law Lords on the 17th. If William thought that the use of an ancient law would afford him justice for the savage violation and murder of his sister, he was terribly wrong. When Abraham was asked whether he was guilty or not his counsel handed him a slip of paper from which he read out: 'Not guilty, and I am ready to defend the same with my body.'

Mr Reader then handed him a pair of gauntlets, one of which he put on, the other he threw down in front of William Ashford.

Abraham had claimed Trial by Wager of Battle, another Norman law.

The Wager of Battle would have seen the two of them agree a date and place for combat, each armed with a staff or club and, basically, fight it out from dawn until the stars appeared in the evening sky. If the guilty person submitted, he would be hanged and if he was killed in the battle, then it was obvious that he really was guilty. However, if he won the battle he must be judged innocent. Abraham Thornton was one of the fittest and strongest men in Warwickshire. William Ashford was described as dwarfish and puny. He wouldn't have stood a chance in a battle like this. Not surprisingly, William refused to pick up the gauntlet.

The Law Lords argued over what to do for several months, but in the end, although the law was archaic, it was still on the statute books, and they had to let Abraham go free a second time. They very hastily got the law cancelled afterwards.

Abraham returned to Castle Bromwich, but his life was made a misery by all the gossip. He moved to Liverpool, trying to get passage to America and a new life. This wasn't as simple as he had hoped either; the crew and passengers of the SS *Independence* refused to let him on board; with his history they all thought he would be a 'Jonah' and cause the ship to flounder in a storm. It was two years before his notoriety faded when he left the country on the SS *Shamrock*. He managed to start a new life in Baltimore, running fishing boats, and eventually died in the 1860s at a place called Black Hawk Hall. Rumour has it that he had written a confession to be sent to Castle Bromwich after he was out of the jurisdiction of the English law. This confession was supposed to have been stolen by a prostitute that he visited just before boarding the *Shamrock*. Perhaps she thought she could blackmail him with it, but it was never handed to the police, so it may just be an unsubstantiated rumour. Another rumour that circulated fifty years later was that he had left a deathbed confession with his new wife and family in America. Once again, there is no evidence for this.

The question remains, did Abraham Thornton rape and kill Mary Ashford? The evidence seems conclusive, but there are enough nagging questions to warrant a deeper look. Mary and Abraham spent at least two hours together in the fields at the end of the footpath off Bell Lane. John Umpage had heard them for a good part of that time and thought nothing suspicious was happening. When Mary went back to Hannah's house she tried to deceive her about where she had been, saying that she had spent the night at her grandfather's house. The map of the chase, much quoted in the press at the time, shows a trail of footsteps covering several hundred yards, with sections of running, dodging and walking. If Mary was running in terror from a demented attacker on her way home from Hannah's, she would have had immense trouble in the long dress she was wearing; in those days a woman had to pick up her skirts to run, and at that point she was carrying a bundle of clothes and shopping. She would have had to discard that in order to be able to run for her life. However, if Mary and Abraham were larking about in the field before she went to Hannah's house, there was no bundle of clothes to impede a game of 'kiss chase'. The famous trail of footprints may well have been laid down in the field hours before the fatal incident. During this early part of the night the young couple may well have just been playing about, but left evidence that would later be interpreted as part of a far more sinister event. If Abraham, arguably the strongest and most athletic man in the county, had intended to catch Mary, he would have done it within tens of feet, not hundreds of yards. In those skirts she wouldn't have stood a chance.

The real key to the mystery lies between the tree where the rape was supposed to have taken place and the fatal pit. It is not beyond imagining that Mary and Abraham arranged to meet there after she had collected her belongings from Hannah's, and that is where everything went dreadfully wrong. The evidence of the heavy footprint at the edge of the pit is pretty damning. Abraham seems to have been the person who threw her into the pit where she drowned. However, if this was a premeditated plan to hide the evidence, why on earth did he leave her bundle, bonnet and shoes so highly visible on the bank; surely they would have been thrown into the pit too. Such an oversight suggests Abraham was panicking.

The surgeon's report states that Mary was a virgin before that night, but it also mentions that she was just starting a heavy period. The surgeon suggested that the prolonged dancing session had probably triggered menstruation. Not only had she been dancing all night, but she had skipped supper at Hannah's, and walked into Birmingham with a stock of garden produce that morning; she must have been exhausted. If the two of them made love under that old oak tree, there would have been blood all over the place, and if she fainted because of the shock, he could have assumed she was dead. He may then have panicked, picked her up by the arms, carried her to the pit and chucked in what he thought was a lifeless corpse. The distracted man then ran home across the fields. If he was as fit as everyone said he was, he would have covered the three or four miles in less than half an hour. Back at the edge of the pit lay the abandoned bundle of clothes and a pair of bloodstained shoes that had fallen from Mary's feet as he heaved her into the water. The poor girl awakening only long enough to realise she was drowning.

The jury found Abraham innocent of murder, but I wonder if they would have found him guilty of manslaughter?

CHAPTER 2

The Wicked Robbery of Mr Painter
1835

Like a bunch of hyenas, they quickly ran around to the other end of the street ...

Although the countryside around Birmingham was still green, the city centre could be a dark and ruthless place as early as 1835. In the alleys and streets of the old town there lurked gangs of pickpockets and thugs waiting to prey on the weak and defenceless. There was little in the way of an organised police force, and handful of constables using an archaic system of justice attempted to keep some kind of order. They could still be an effective force because most people knew

Beggars and pickpockets viewed the gentry as easy pickings. R K Dent

and respected their attempts to keep the city peaceful and safe. This was an era where everyone felt that they were part of the social order and had to play their part in the community, apart from the villains of course.

William Painter was a well respected gentleman who had moved to Ravenhurst Street in Aston from the little country village of Snitterfield near Warwick. He was sixty years old and lived in the house with his daughter, Caroline Charlotte. He was a tax collector and regularly travelled about the city collecting the assessed taxes from the few people eligible to pay them. In those days income tax and the like was restricted to substantially well off people, and, believe it or not, some of them even volunteered to pay it! On Monday afternoon, 16 February, William left his house as usual to conduct his business in the city.

In an altogether different part of the city, Parke Street, a gang of villains were getting ready to conduct their less savoury business. The gang was centred around William Dollman, who, at twenty-nine years old, was the most experienced. His main crony was Nathaniel Hedge, a twenty-one-year-old who had already been in trouble with the law. A shifty character called William Knowles and a young lad of only fifteen, John Gough, completed the gang. They all met together in the late afternoon at the *Duke of Cumberland* pub in Parke Street and sat around drinking ale and discussing what to do that day. After a pint or two they decided to go up to the Playhouse and see what they could get from picking a few pockets.

At the gallery door of the Playhouse they got an unpleasant surprise. One of the Street Keepers, with his bright red-collared uniform, was keeping watch. The gang ducked out of sight and furtively made their way around to the Theatre of Arts in New Street. They had no better luck there; Constable Hall was on duty by the door. Frustrated, they made their way up Temple Street to *Dee's Hotel* beside the churchyard in Temple Row. It was here that Gough spotted Mr Painter.

'Here's a nice old fellow, let's follow him.'

'I shan't go,' said Knowles.

'Come on!' retorted Dollman and the gang followed Mr Painter down Cherry Street, Union Street and into Union Passage. Here, the four crooks arranged that the three men

EXECUTION OF
WILLIAM DOLLMAN AND NATHANIEL HEDGE
FOR THE MURDER OF MR. PAINTER.

The unhappy culprits were found guilty, on Thursday, the 2nd instant, of the wilful murder of Mr. Painter, at Birmingham, on the 23d of February last. *John Gough*, a lad of 15 or 16, was condemned at the same time, having been convicted of assisting in the perpetration of the murder, but was reprieved on Friday morning by the Judge before he left the town.

A contemporary newspaper headline. Warwickshire Advertiser

would jostle the old man whilst the lad Gough would sneak up and snatch his watch. They tracked him down New Street and into Worcester Street. Like a bunch of hyenas, they quickly ran around to the other end of the street hoping to waylay him as he emerged from the alley into Parsonage Ground.

The plan was hastily changed as Mr Painter turned off into an alley under a stable wall. Knowles stood guard at the alley entrance and the other three approached him. Dollman swung his fist at the old man, missed completely, and fell into a pile of horse muck.

'What did you do that for?' asked the shocked old man.

'I'll tell you what I did that for, you old bugger,' said Dollman, and took another swing, hitting him hard on the jaw this time. Mr Painter jerked back against the wall and fell forward to the ground.

'There's a man watching us,' Knowles called out and the gang scattered, John Gough staying the longest to try to get the watch, but with no success. Mr Painter shoved him away. Dollman and Knowles sprinted around to the back of the alley and met up with Gough. What they hadn't realised was that Hedges quickly returned, grabbed Mr Painter by the throat, hit him again on the jaw and rolled him over to get at his watch and then left hurriedly after kicking him a few times out of sheer malice.

Mr Painter struggled to his feet, bleeding badly from his cuts and bruises, and in agony from a broken jaw. He staggered to the end of the alley, trying to do up his buttons and made his

way unsteadily down Hurst Street and into a pub on the corner
of Bromsgrove Street. The three villains watched him reach
safety and went back to the stables to see if anything valuable
had been dropped in the scuffle.

There was nothing to salvage and as the three of them walked
back to the *Duke of Cumberland,* Gough said he reckoned
Nathaniel Hedge must have got the watch. Once they got there,
Hedge was sitting in the kitchen looking smug.

'You've got the watch, haven't you?'

'Yes, I had to roll the old bugger over two or three times to
get it.'

'Where is it?' asked Gough.

'It's up in Freeman Street.' Bill Knowles went with Hedges to
his mother's house to get the watch.

It was at about this time the Mr Painter was brought home on
the back of Mr Hartle's cart. He was in a very sorry state: his hat
smashed, clothes ripped and filthy, blood pouring from his
mouth. Caroline took him upstairs, put him to bed and called
the surgeon, Mr John Wright. Wright did what he could to
make William comfortable, but the poor man was in agony,
barely able to speak and virtually unable to swallow. His jaw
and throat were already beginning to swell up from the extens-
ive bruising and fracture on the left side.

Back at the *Duke of Cumberland,* the gang examined their
haul. The watch was a valuable one, with a silver double case. It
was attached to a key and a couple of seals with a black ribbon.
Quite how to convert the watch and seals to cash was a problem
they would have to leave until tomorrow. A little after 10.00 pm
the gang went around to Knowles' lodgings and hid the watch
under a loose hearthstone. Dollman and Knowles went to bed
and Hedges and Gough went home.

Early the next day, Knowles and Dollman went back to the
scene of the robbery once again. They were sure that some
money must have been dropped there. All they got for their
pains was a very long hard stare from Constable Hall. The
whole gang met up at the *Painter Arms* in London Prentice
Street. Here, they met Benjamin Jones of Suffolk Street, their
fence. Knowles and Dollman agreed with him that he would sell
the watch for as much as he could get, giving them twenty-five
shillings, and keeping anything over that for himself.

Knowles and Jones went up to the *Hole in the Wall* in Bordesley Street. Benjamin Jones wasn't just any old crooked fence, but an amateur boxer too. He had a sparring match with another customer of the pub, Thomas Griffiths, a grinder from Sun Street. Amid the shouts and excitement of the boxing bout in the bar some more people expressed an interest in the watch. By 2 o'clock in the afternoon a small band of petty criminals set off from the *Hole in the Wall* to get the watch valued by Henry Watkins, watchmaker, of Cheapside. There was Henry Cramer riding his horse. Knowles had offered him the watch for £2, the two Fanthom brothers, sons of the landlord of the *Hole in the Wall*, Mr Daniel, Thomas Griffiths and Knowles himself. Knowles had such a dodgy reputation that he gave the watch to Griffiths to take it into the shop.

Knowles and most of the motley crew went into the *Cross Keys Inn* whilst Griffiths and Benjamin Jones got the watch valued. It may not have been valued that highly because of a chip on the enamel face. It was a blemish that Caroline Painter had attempted to mend her self by applying a little paint to it. It was a mark that uniquely identified the watch. Caroline herself was now beside herself with worry. Her father could neither eat nor drink, and an infection was setting into the cuts and fracture of his jaw. He was an extremely ill man.

Griffiths kept the watch when they came out of the shop. He may well have intended to keep it for himself because on their return to town he went into the prison, knowing full well that the rest of the petty criminals would never follow him in there. Knowles had to admit to Dollman that he no longer had the watch. Not surprisingly, Dollman was furious; he now only had the key and seals to show for the robbery.

That evening Knowles managed to sell the seals for just one shilling and the promise of a puppy from another shady character by the name of Henry Hart, of Shutt Lane. The puppy wouldn't have been some cute floppy eared softie, there was a thriving trade in fighting dogs amid the underworld of the day, mastiff-type dogs were worth a fortune if they fought well. They kept the constables at a distance too. In one police raid the constables had to shoot the dogs before they could get to the house.

John Gough was annoyed that he didn't seem to be getting his share of the spoils.

William Painter was fading fast. On Wednesday the infection spread from his jaw and throat to his lungs, and on the Thursday morning he died. The constable's search was no longer for a stolen watch but a gang of murderers. Sergeant Redfern had already heard plenty of rumours about who was responsible and on Friday arrested Knowles and Dollman. Over the weekend, most of the others were picked up. Thomas Griffiths wisely handed over the watch, pretending he knew nothing of its origins, whilst Henry Hart threw the seals onto his fire and destroyed them.

The trial took place on 4 April. William Knowles had made a full and damning confession in the hope of being spared the death sentence. It worked, and only Dollman, Hedge and Gough were charged with the murder of William Painter. The court at Warwick was packed with people not only from Birmingham, but many from Mr Painter's home village of Snitterfield too. The case took the entire day to cover, ending with the death sentence being passed on the three men at around 8 o'clock in the evening. Dollman swore he was innocent and Knowles had made the whole thing up. Hedge said

The original prison in Peck Lane has long since vanished beneath the site of New Street Station. R K Dent

nothing and the young John Gough burst into tears begging for mercy and saying he was 'as innocent as a lamb'.

John Gough's youth saved him from the gallows. He was reprieved but Hedge and Dollman had to face the full rigour of English justice. They had a few days to receive visits from their family and make their peace with God. Hedge was a Roman Catholic, Dollman, an Anglican. The following Saturday saw them hanged in front of Warwick Gaol. They maintained a degree of dignity to the end. Neither of them confessed to the murder, but then they didn't deny it either. Their execution was quick, they were placed side by side on the gallows and, this being 1835, were strangled by the noose within a couple of minutes of the drop. This was the era of the short drop, the victims being tipped off a plank and dropping only a foot or two. It was a pretty barbaric way to execute someone, but no more barbaric than the way old Mr Painter met his end. This was justice very much being seen to be done. Thousands of people had walked all the way from Birmingham to watch the spectacle. There were stands selling refreshments, and even though it was mid-morning quite a few of the crowd were drunk

Birmingham's Theatre of Arts attracted a wealthy clientele, just what a gang of pickpockets needed. R K Dent

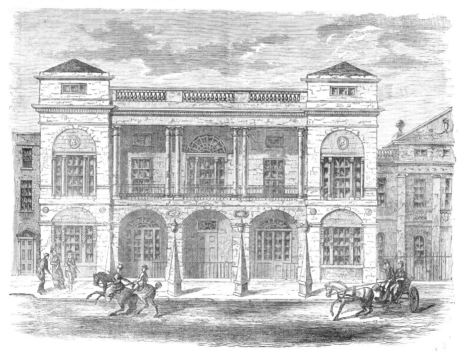

and raucous. As the men ascended the scaffold a cry went up: 'Hats!', to tell the people at the front to stop blocking the view with their hats, nothing to do with respect for the condemned men.

It was a grisly entertainment that offended the sensibilities of many of the gentry and, after the mass hangings of the last century, when you could be hung for stealing a side of bacon, a movement was already starting for the abolition of the death penalty.

Chapter 3

William Devey
1838

*There was an ear-splitting crash as
the gun went off.*

In the 1830s, Birmingham was just starting to become the centre of English engineering. Vast factories had sprung up in the north of England making textiles, but engineering was a craft and skill that didn't lend itself to mass production until later in the nineteenth century. Birmingham was filled with hundreds of small workshops employing just a few staff. Little Hampton Street was fairly typical. It comprised of reasonably-sized workshops, some with living accommodation above the shop floor, others with steam powered mills. From these workshops came all manner of products: cutlery, guns, and buttons; if you wanted it then someone would make it. It was all thirsty work and the whole community, from workers to bosses, quenched their thirst at *The Pheasant*.

George Askey was a die-sinker, a highly skilled craftsman capable of making the dies that made anything from pierced metal to spoons. His story was common enough; after he had served his seven year apprenticeship he spent a while working on his own account but couldn't raise enough capital to get his own workshop. On 8 November 1836, he decided he would take up a full time job with Rowley, Stamper & Piercer. It wasn't what he was used to as his own man; the hours were from 7 o'clock to 7 o'clock in the summer, with a couple of hours for breaks, and from 8 o'clock to 7 o'clock in the winter, but with just one hour for a break, six days a week. The position was well paid since there were so few people with those skills. Mr Rowley seems to have been a fairly long-suffering employer – until pushed too far.

William Devey was one of the many workshop owners who had employed George Askey from time to time when he worked for himself, and found it most exceedingly inconvenient that he could no longer rely on his skills once he started his new job. George told him right away that he was no longer free; he was now an articled servant. George had no tools, and was loathe to break the terms of his employment. William Devey wheedled and begged repeatedly until George eventually relented and agreed to do just a few days for him. Devey's business was making silver plated spoons but without accurate dies he could not stamp out and shape the metal blanks. Devey himself was only twenty-eight and had been running the business since he was about twenty. He was 5 feet 9 inches tall, well built and was married with two young children. The factory used the dies to stamp out thousands of teaspoons, having cast the blanks first and then plated the resulting spoons. Devey had recently introduced steam power to run the stamping machines by renting power from the steam engine in George Leeson's factory next door. The factory was its own little community, with Devey and his family living on the premises together with their housemaid, Lydia Tucker. Every morning about a dozen labourers turned up and, until now, it had all gone very well indeed. The introduction of steam had sped up the production, but of course it had added an extra cost to the business, and that was something Devey hadn't anticipated accurately.

Through December 1836 and January 1837, George went half a dozen times to Devey's workshop, mending and renewing the all important dies. Mostly he went late at night so that he was not breaking his terms of work with Mr Rowley. By March, the pressure of work at Devey's was so great that he was being woken at 4 o'clock in the morning by William and then being pressured to stay on long after he should have started at Mr Rowley's. It didn't take long for Devey to persuade George to stay a couple of days, sending a message to Mr Rowley that he was sick. What probably finally drove the long suffering Mr Rowley wild with rage was that George had learnt several of his techniques for improving the stamping process, and introduced those into William Devey's factory.

Mr Rowley listened to the gossip in *The Pheasant* and realised what was going on: his most skilled workman was moonlighting with one of his competitors. In February, Rowley told Devey to stop employing him or he would sue. George had to spend the whole night in the workshop because Rowley was out looking for him. Devey was seriously worried about Mr Rowley's threat to sue him; it was a serious offence to entice a hired servant away from their lawful master. It was time for a little insurance policy. In April, he managed to get the hapless George Askey totally drunk, then persuaded him to stagger up the road to Mr Smith's house in Aston Street and swear that he had never worked for him. He was that drunk that he remembered nothing of the event. Devey was proving a devious business-man.

In May, George Askey was finally hauled up before the magistrates and imprisoned for a month for neglecting his proper job. Serious questions were raised about William Devey's business methods. Askey managed to convince William that he should at least pay ten shillings a week to his wife whilst he was in prison, or he could give some pretty damning evidence against him. Devey did so, though hardly with the best will. Luckily Mr Rowley had forgiven Askey for his mis-demeanours since he promised never to work for Devey again and would work regularly in future.

George Askey was true to his word and, despite all the wheedling William Devey could manage, he never set foot in his workshop again. This was just one more problem for the spoon making business. William Devey was losing production and sales as well as facing a law suit from Mr Rowley regarding the costs involved in his using Askey's labour during Rowley's time. Devey was getting increasingly paranoid as the pressure of his failing business piled up on top of him. He tried to get Askey to swear an oath that he had never worked for him. That wasn't going to work because George refused to swear a false oath. Devey then tried to set up a charade where his brother John paid him for some fake bills George was told to submit, but then insisted that George give him the money back: 'Now Askey, if you should be called as a witness against me you can safely swear that you have worked for John and not me, and he paid you for it.'

The ploy might have worked if he had let George keep the money, he was still out of pocket from his month long stay in prison. As it was, William Devey was losing his grip on things. One of his best friends was the landlord of *The Pheasant*,

Mr Davenport. Over the years they had spent many pleasant evenings talking away in the pub, but now those days were over and their relationship cooled as William suspected that the garrulous landlord was letting slip just how much financial difficulty he was getting into.

In December 1837, increasingly desperate for money, William made the mistake of trying to sue Askey for the money he had paid to his wife whilst he was in prison, all forty shillings of it. The case appears to have been thrown out of the Court of Requests, but it persuaded Askey to act as prime witness in Mr Rowley's law suit. This was set to take place in March 1838.

By then, Devey was in serious financial trouble. He owed three months' payments to his neighbour George Leeson for the mill power he rented from him to power his stamping machines. He also owed a substantial amount to the gas company. His mood of desperation was made worse by the result of the court case at the Warwick assizes. The judge found Devey's behaviour was unacceptable and awarded damages of forty shillings against him. The case was heard on Friday 30 March and reported in the local papers the following day. It was, naturally, the talk of *The Pheasant* for the whole weekend.

It wasn't only in *The Pheasant* that news of the case aroused interest. Mr Redfern of the gas company read the article on Saturday and decided that since Devey owed the company for three months' gas supply he had better take steps to cover the company's interests. He directed William White, a policeman for the Liverpool Railway Company, to enter Devey's premises and distrain his goods. This was to ensure that neither Devey nor anyone else could take them away until the gas company had been paid its bill. William White had little choice but to join the household, having dinner with them each evening. Devey suggested that he could have one or two of the stamping machines in lieu of payment, but the machines weighed several tons each and there was no way that the man could move them. On the Tuesday evening, Devey was called around to George Leeson's warehouse next door but one. He too, wanted his money. They talked for a fair while, Devey complaining that Davenport had told the gas company about his difficulties, how the man had become his greatest enemy while he had remained

William Devey's troubles began at the Court of Requests, and ended on the gallows.
R K Dent

his greatest friend. Leeson told him how he must be mistaken and that Davenport would never hurt a soul. William Devey was still convinced that Joseph Davenport had sent word to the gas company that he was moving his goods out of the warehouse and this had caused them to send in the bailiff. Devey seems to have been descending into a paranoid delusion. Lydia Tucker was convinced that his behaviour had changed since the

A common pistol of the era, cocked and ready to fire. These pistols had a folding trigger so that they could be safely carried in a pocket. They held just one bullet and were loaded by unscrewing the barrel to insert the shot and powder. At short range they were completely lethal. Arbour Antiques

defeat in court. Isaac Hope was the plater for the business and he too thought Devey was buckling under the pressure of several law suits, financial pressures and his own rather over excitable nature.

Frederick Watson turned up for work at Devey's workshop as usual on Wednesday. Devey was fussing about and told him to stick close to his work. He might have to go out of the way for a time. He was worried sick after the exposure in the *Gazette* as a near bankrupt. At about 3.00 pm, he went out and Frederick could finally relax.

Emma Davis was the next person to see him. She was behind the counter of the gun shop that she and her sister ran in Bull Street. Devey asked for a pair of common pistols. Emma showed him a pair that were priced at 10s 6d. It was pretty clear to her that he had no idea how to use the firearms and she had to show him how to work them, repeatedly loading with powder, fitting the little copper percussion caps and firing blank shots into the back workshop. William bought the pair of pistols, saying that they were for a friend of his in Solihull. She told him he would have to wait for an hour whilst they made half a pound of bullets, as they had run out of the right size.

Freshly-cast bullets. Caroline Webley had to cast the bullets specially for William Devey using a mould. Arbour Antiques

Devey went home rather than wait in the shop. Isaac Hope heard him talking to his wife at 3.30 pm: 'Make yourself as comfortable as you can,' he told her, 'I must be going somewhere.' Isaac got the distinct feeling that Devey intended to kill himself.

At 4.00 pm Devey returned to the gunshop and Caroline Webley gave him the twenty-eight bullets that her sister had just cast for him. He walked back towards Little Hampton Street. As he passed the *Salutation Inn and Liquor Store* he met his old friend Benjamin Clulee coming out. Benjamin was the steam mill engineer at Snow Hill; he had advised William not to use rented steam power for his stamping machines. William said: 'Well old friend Clulee, I am glad to see thee, you shall go in and have a glass along with me.'

Benjamin was tempted back into the pub and William bought him a glass of gin. He had nothing for himself. When he pulled out his money a couple of pennies dropped to the floor.

'I'm not quite ruined yet,' he said, as he looked at a few sovereigns in his hand. 'What do you think of that damned thief Davenport writing to my creditors to tell them if they meant to have anything they must come in immediately?'

Benjamin said he didn't think Davenport would do any such thing.

'I'm a ruined man, and it's that man that has ruined me!'

Benjamin Clulee calmly told Devey that he should stop pursuing so many law suits and such like.

'I will have my revenge,' said William.

'Revenge be damned,' Clulee told him, 'you will never go on in this course of life to do any good.'

Devey looked at him strangely, saying: 'My things will be sold in a few days but my affairs will soon be settled. They will be very shortly settled.' His face fell into a distant expression.

Benjamin thought William looked ill and suggested he took a glass of wine. Devey would not touch it though. Benjamin left the distracted man to his own devices and left. James Spittle, the local policeman called into the pub at 5.30 pm and spent a while passing the time of day with William, but he noticed nothing strange about him at that time.

By 7 o'clock, Frederick Watson was finished for the day. He packed up his tools and went down to the entrance of the warehouse. Outside, he saw Mr Davenport walking along in the middle of the road, and some ten yards behind him was William Devey, still wearing his white apron, and walking with his hands in his pockets. They were both walking towards Mr Batkin's locksmith's shop. Frederick noticed nothing unusual and casually wandered off home.

Joseph Davenport went into Mr Batkin's. George Leeson was standing by his door and noticed William Devey walk past the shop door, then quickly turn upon his heel, and follow Joseph in. George felt something was very wrong and started running across the road towards the shop.

Samuel Farrington was standing in the shop when Davenport entered and asked to see Mr Batkin. Samuel went out to the rear workshop to call him. He returned in less than a minute and, just as he did so, Devey came in through the street door. He went straight up to Davenport, shouting: 'Damn your eyes, you have been the ruin of me.'

'What do you follow me for?' asked the perplexed Mr Davenport.

'Now I will settle you!' came the reply.

Devey raised his right arm, as though to strike Joseph, and Samuel was staggered to see that he was holding a small black gun. There was an ominous click, but no explosion. Perhaps Joseph thought he might be spared as he rushed to the door of Mr Batkin's parlour, bumping into Samuel in his rush. Samuel saw Devey put his arm down, then raise it once more, pointing another pistol at Joseph's head. There was an ear-splitting crash as the gun went off. Stone dead, Joseph collapsed onto Samuel, knocking him to the floor and pinning him there.

George Leeson came through the door just as Devey fired the fatal shot. Samuel struggled to push the body off and stand up. Devey was muttering: 'Take me now, take me now.' He walked towards the door.

Leeson grabbed him by the collar, saying: 'Come, Devey, this game will never do.'

'Very well, you may do what you like with me, Mr Leeson,' was Devey's response.

Devey threw a pistol towards the gutter in the street, and then dropped another at George's feet. George bent down to pick it up, still keeping hold of William's collar.

James Webb was immediately in front of the shop door and saw Devey pulling off his neckerchief, whereupon he said: 'I resign myself; I shall die happy,' and with this he started to hack at his own bare throat with a knife.

As George straightened up with the gun in his hand, he realised that Devey had pulled out a wickedly sharp cobbler's knife and was attempting to cut his own throat. Both George and James Webb tried to wrestle the knife away from Devey, but there was blood flying everywhere. More people joined the struggle and Devey was overpowered. George had his collar,

Devey was rushed to the General Hospital to treat the wounds on his neck after his suicide attempt. R K Dent

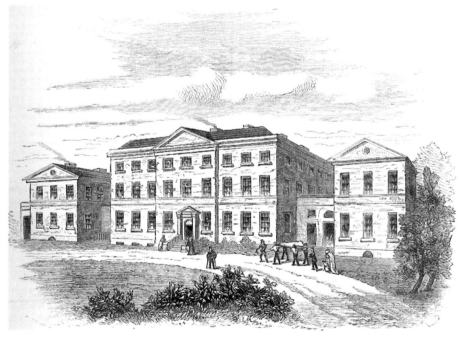

James his arms. Devey struggled for a while but was rapidly weakening from loss of blood. He may have missed all the major blood vessels, but he had slashed many of the small ones, and cut open his windpipe, too.

'Finish me, finish me,' he gasped.

William Devey was quickly taken to the hospital. It was all too late for Joseph Davenport. The bullet had penetrated the left side of his skull and travelled right through his brain, shattering the bone on the right side. He had died instantly. His body was carried back to *The Pheasant*.

In the hospital the surgeon examined Devey's cut throat. Cheerfully, he remarked that it wasn't all that bad.

'I hope not,' Devey said, 'for I shall be hanged. I have murdered a man. I shot him ... Let me die ... Let me die.'

William Devey did not die, but once he was fit enough he was taken to Warwick Gaol to await trial at the August assizes. His optimism returned briefly and he even made an attempt to escape, but once caught he collapsed back into a state of abject dejection. He even refused to go to church. By the time his case came up, on 10 August, he was quite resigned to die. Just as

One of the cell doors of Warwick Gaol has been preserved in Barrack Street, Warwick. Perhaps it is the one that incarcerated William Devey. Author's collection

BIRMINGHAM.

HORRIBLE MURDER AND ATTEMPT AT SUICIDE.

In our paper of Saturday last we mentioned a frightful case of murder, arising from feelings of resentment and revenge, committed on the previous Wednesday night, by a man named William Devey, a spoonmaker, of Little Hampton-street, on Mr. Joseph Davenport, landlord of the "Pheasant" public-house, in the same street. It now appears that Devey committed the dreadful crime in the most cool and premeditated manner. He has lately fallen into difficulties, and he supposed, most incorrectly as it appears, that Davenport, his neighbour, had given information of the embarrassed state of his circumstances to some of his creditors, who had put bailiffs into his house. Brooding over the supposed injury done him by Davenport, the misguided man determined to satisfy his thirst for revenge by murder and self-destruction at the

Extract from the Warwickshire Advertiser *concerning the sensational case.*
Warwickshire Advertiser

well really, because the jury had no qualms about finding him guilty of wilful murder, and the judge spent a good while lecturing about how he richly deserved to go to the gallows.

In the short time before his execution was due William had several very distressing meetings with his wife and family. She could not understand how things had gone from such a prosperous business to the death cell in so short a time. A petition was raised in Birmingham begging that the death sentence be commuted and even the local papers started a campaign against capital punishment as an inhuman and barbarous method of dealing with criminals. It was to achieve nothing.

On Friday 24 August, William Devey stepped up on to the scaffold. He was wearing a light shooting jacket, dark stripped trousers and a black neckerchief. In front of him was a crowd of several thousand, in a very festive mood. The turnkey gave him a glass of wine before pinioning his arms to his side. A cry of 'Hats!' went up to persuade the people at the front of the crowds to take off their hats so that the people at the back could see better. William Devey dropped, and was no more.

As his body dangled on the end of the rope, a dozen or so women pushed their way through the crowd and rubbed his

Warwick Gaol gates, the scene of many executions in the early nineteenth century. Public executions continued until 1868. Author's collection

dead hand against their swollen necks. The touch of an executed man's hand was a well known cure for the affliction called 'wens', a swelling of the thyroid and neck. After an hour he was cut down and buried in the prison yard.

CHAPTER 4

Matthew Davies
1848

She managed three steps across the yard before collapsing onto the cobbles.

e understand quite a lot about head injuries and their effects these days; no doubt there is plenty more to learn, but we've a reasonable idea about what is involved. There are antibiotics, surgery, therapies of all sorts. More importantly, there is the chance of a diagnosis before matters get out of control. This was not the case in the 1840s.

Matthew Davies took a hefty blow to the back of his head from a constable's staff sometime around 1846. It left him with a scar to his dying day. This was an age where some medics believed that the bumps and the shape of the skull determined the behaviour and character of their patients. Mr Birt of Leamington Spa, a senior assistant at the Whitley Lunatic Asylum, thought the wound on Matthew's head would predispose him to insanity. Dr Hansom of the Hanwell Asylum agreed and stated that anyone with a skull of that construction would show suicidal tendencies. This was all a bit academic. By the time Matthew's skull was examined he was on trial for his life.

After the injury Matthew's behaviour changed towards the erratic. He started to grind his teeth, clench his fists at random

Matthew Davies. Warwickshire Advertiser

MURDER.

Matthew Davies, (42) who was described in the calendar as being enabled to read and write well, was then arranged upon a charge of having murdered his wife, Mary Davies, on the 13th of October last, by cutting her throat in a ferocious manner. The precincts of the Court were crowded at an early hour by that class of persons who are ever anxious to feed upon the wonderful and bloody, and amongst the mass might be observed an immense number of females. Upon the prisoner being arranged he pleaded not guilty in a very tremulous voice, and appeared during the trial to breathe oppressively. He was dressed in deep mourning, and appeared to be acutely alive to the awful position in which he stood. He was a strong built man, with a countenance rather expressing an indication of mildness than otherwise. He was defended by Mr. Macaulay and Mr. Miller; Mr. Willmore conducting the prosecution.

moments. He would suddenly grin wildly at nothing. A friend of his, Elizabeth Hughes, noticed him complaining about his head and remembered how he would suddenly stand up calling 'Hush, hush', putting his hands over his ears, when the room was completely quiet. Another friend had regularly seen him batter his fists against each other in such a fury that they swelled to twice their normal size. Matthew Davies was in a mess.

Matthew did not live an asylum though, he ran a restaurant in Moor Street and his eccentric behaviour soon attracted attention and further problems. The young men working in the bedstead factory behind the restaurant would occasionally spot him drunk and poke fun at him, calling him 'Mad Davies', then rub Raddle, the metal cleaning polish, over his clothes. Perhaps not surprisingly, Matthew increasingly turned to the bottle. Through 1847 the bouts of insanity and drunkenness increased. At one point Matthew called a bailiff to clear the customers out of the restaurant. James Dunnifer got them out, but then found Matthew virtually hysterical and together with some others had to confine him in an upstairs room. They had to nail the windows shut to stop Matthew jumping out.

Mary Davies, his wife, could only take so much. Matthew started smashing up the furniture in temper tantrums. At one point he even set fire to the house. The trouble was that after the tantrum passed he seemed to know nothing of what had happened. Quarrels between the two of them became an almost incessant battle. Through 1847 Mary bore as much as she

Moor Street, long before the railways arrived. Author's collection

could, but there was a limit. Their next door neighbour, Mary Machell, often saw the rows, the smashed furniture and broken glass. Sadly, she also saw the way that afterwards the bemused and confused man ran to his wife to embrace and kiss her, seeking some kind of stability in an increasingly alien world. Elizabeth Hughes also noticed how very fond and doting Matthew was with his wife. By October 1847, Mary Davies had had enough. It was her that had the shorter temper now, Matthew's erratic behaviour sparking a tirade of abuse and vilification. Something was set to snap. Mary took out a summons against Matthew. She planned to leave him.

On the morning of 13 October, Matthew and Mary, together with their charwoman, Eliza Yarneld, were in the kitchen of the restaurant preparing for another busy day. Matthew was peeling the potatoes and Mary was washing her hands with soap and a flannel. The summons was the topic of conversation. Eliza had already seen Matthew go down on his knees and beg Mary not to leave, tears pouring down his cheeks.

'If you won't go, Mary, I'll be tidy,' he pleaded, and then suddenly his mood changed.

'Such damned nonsense', he muttered as he drew the paring knife across the sharpening steel five times.

'I will go if God spare me,' she retorted angrily.

'Damn your eyes, you shan't go.' Matthew stood up.

'I'll give you a slap of the face if you don't go on with your nonsense.'

'Damn your eyes, you shan't go.'

Eliza watched him go up to Mary and put his left arm around her neck as though he was going to kiss her. Blood gushed up into the air. Eliza fled through the back door screaming for help. As she turned back, Mary staggered through the door and out into the yard, her hands clutching her throat in a futile attempt to stop the blood spraying through her fingers. She managed three steps across the yard before collapsing onto the cobbles.

Matthew walked over to the kitchen fire and stood casually with his back to it as though nothing at all had happened.

Henrietta Hughes and Constable Bees had responded to Eliza's frantic calls. Henrietta arrived just as Mary fell to the ground, still clutching her slashed throat. Seconds later,

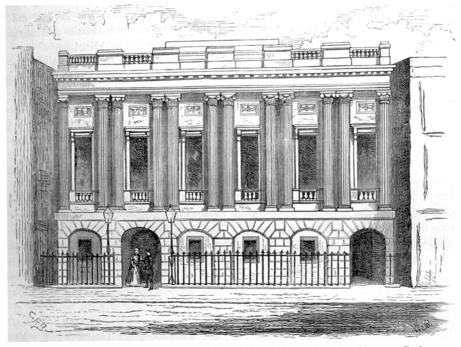

The Borough built a new gaol and offices in New Street when the old one at Peck Lane became too small to cope with all the criminals. R K Dent

Constable Bees arrived. He spotted Matthew wandering out of the kitchen door, his right hand covered in blood.

'What's the matter? What's the matter?' Matthew seemed unaware that he had just cut his wife's throat.

The constable grabbed Matthew by the collar.

'Don't pull me,' he snarled.

The surgeon arrived as the constable took Matthew away. There was nothing to be done for Mary, she had bled to death in a few minutes. Matthew had ripped a huge gash across her throat, severing the arteries and windpipe.

Matthew was brought to trial at Warwick in April the following year. He was dressed in mourning clothes and appeared to be a nervous wreck. There was little that he could do to defend himself and, although his counsel produced a lot of evidence to indicate his insanity, it wasn't enough to convince the jury or judge. He was condemned to death and hanged on the gallows a fortnight later. His body was cut down after an hour and buried in an unmarked grave within the confines of Warwick Gaol.

CHAPTER 5

Mary Turner
1860

She burst out of the back door, rushed across the yard and ... shot him.

Although many of these ghastly tales seem to involve women being variously abused and murdered by unspeakably stupid men, it should never be assumed that Birmingham women were poor little things who never fought back. This was something that William White discovered to his cost in 1860.

William White was considered a cad by pretty much everyone who met him, apart from a poor nineteen-year-old orphan girl from Kidderminster. Mary Turner was left alone after her mother died and White started walking out with her. Within a few months he had managed to persuade her that he would marry her eventually, and she moved in with him at his lodgings.

Over the next eighteen months their domestic life as man and wife was punctuated by several rows. Mrs Onions, their landlady, had to step in between them on various occasions when White started to beat Mary. It wasn't a perfect relationship, and White started to eye up other young girls.

By April 1860, not only had White found himself another girlfriend, despite Mary living with him at Mrs Onions, Mary herself seems to have thought she was pregnant and visited a doctor. A flaming row broke out and White told Mary that he was going to marry the other girl instead. After the row, life in the house descended into a sullen silence. Mary refused to speak to White and moved into another room.

A few weeks passed and White managed to make matters worse by starting a rumour that Mary had got pregnant with

The centre of Birmingham in Mary Turner's day. Old and New Birmingham

someone else. On one Saturday night he rubbed it all in by taunting Mary about his forthcoming marriage to the new girl. This was the last straw for Mary. She was feeling pretty hard done by to start with, having worked hard to keep their precarious relationship together and then being dumped for her

A typical pistol of the 1860s. The shot and powder are loaded through the muzzle. The hammer now fires a percussion cap instead of a flintlock. The pistol could fire either a bullet or bird shot. William White was lucky that Mary Turner did not know how to load the pistol properly. Arbour Antiques

pains. During the afternoon of 8 May she grew increasingly furious at his cheek.

William White wandered into the yard late that afternoon, and went to the brewhouse to wash himself. He was completely oblivious to Mary's frustration and anger at his treatment of her. She burst out of the back door, rushed across the yard and, to his complete surprise, shot him.

Mary Turner was not one of nature's born killers. She had loaded the pistol with an inadequate charge of gunpowder and very small bore shot. She wasn't a particularly good markswoman either. The blast caught White in the side, the pellets ruining his jacket and shirt but only a few of them penetrated as far as his skin and only a fraction of those embedded themselves in his skin. Mrs Onions looked out of the kitchen window to see White chasing Mary round the garden trying to get the gun off her.

PC Bird heard the shot and turned up in time to catch Mary before White could inflict any revenge on her. He arrested her and said she would be charged with attempted murder.

'I did it, and I would do it again if I got fifteen years for it.'

Not possibly the best defence against the charge, but it was enough to ensure that Mary went to the next session of the Warwick Assizes. William White pressed charges of attempted murder and grievous bodily harm against her.

Mary Turner was not a wealthy woman and she had to rely on the court's own defence counsel to argue her case. Usually this was a cursory and flimsy defence, but in this case everyone was happy to support her. The poor girl fainted when William White was brought in to give his evidence, and even Mr Wills, the prosecution lawyer, started his address by stating how badly White had treated her. Mr O'Brien in her defence summed up the continual abuse, exploitation and the taunts that had led to the final shooting. Even the judge came down on her side.

To William White's astonishment, halfway through the hearing the Judge intervened and said that as far as he could understand the gunshot wound was so trivial that it didn't even amount to grievous bodily harm under the precise terms of the law. Mr O'Brien then insisted that there was no evidence of malice, and that White had caused Mary such personal distress that she was too over excited to know what she was doing.

The judge summed up the case very much in favour of Mary, and even though the jury did find her guilty of attempting to inflict grievous bodily harm on White, they also strongly recommended mercy in view of White's behaviour. All the other charges were dismissed.

History does not record whether they gave her the gun back.

You didn't have to be a wronged woman to get a very light sentence. Some years earlier George Higgs was put on trial at Warwick Assizes. The charge was that he had killed and slayed William Rousham in a field beside the *Kings Head*, Deritend, in November 1843.

During the evening before this dreadful deed, William had attempted to take liberties with George's sister and a fight started off in the bar. Joseph Reeve, the landlord, told the two of them to stop fighting in the bar. At this George said he would happily have a proper fight in a ring with William. William agreed and the following morning a square was roped off in the field, Joseph Reeve acted as referee and second to both of them and they started hammering away at each other in a proper boxing match. Round after round passed as the two equally matched men pummelled each other. After ninety minutes, Joseph was thinking that it might be time to get them to stop. George was holding his own but not making any serious headway against William. William, however, couldn't get in any knockout punches. George also appeared to be getting tired.

In the thirtieth round, or there abouts – no one was properly counting – George managed to get one hefty punch to the side of Willam's head. A couple of seconds later, Willam fell flat on his face, completely unconscious. Several spectators carried him off to the General Hospital and the duty surgeon, W C Freer, examined him. William had a massive bruise on the side of his head, but few other marks from the fight. Inside his skull it was a different matter, his brain had been lacerated by fragments of bone shattered by the blow. Three hours later, William Rousham died and George Higgs was arrested for murder.

It was quite acceptable to settle serious disputes with a proper boxing match. Author's collection

The case came up at the assizes and the details of the fight accurately reported. The jury found Higgs guilty of manslaughter, with a recommendation to the judge for mercy. The judge in his summing up of the case praised George for upholding his sister's honour, his honesty in having a properly refereed fight and gained a round of applause from the public gallery when he sentenced him to three days in prison. Somewhat better than the gallows, I'm sure you'll agree.

CHAPTER 6

Francis Price
1860

There on the floor lay Sarah, her arm just flopping down amid a growing pool of blood.

The course of true love rarely runs smooth, and for a shy young man, Francis Price, it hit the buffers in tragic style.

Francis was only nine when his father died, and just eleven when his mother passed away. It was lucky for him that he had just been found a position as apprentice shoemaker in his hometown of Stafford. Apprenticeships in the 1850s were a very inclusive affair, the young lad getting board and lodgings as well as training; and if he was lucky he would even get pocket money. Some apprentices went on to take over the family business as their master grew old but many fell by the wayside. There were plenty of ruthless characters ready to exploit the young men and repay them nothing for all their years of work.

Francis Price ran away from his apprenticeship before it was officially over. Despite being something of a loner, he managed to start business on his own account as a 'runner', an intermediary between shoemakers and shopkeepers. It was quite successful to start with; Francis travelled to all the major cities of England, making the most of the new railways, finding contacts and business wherever he went. By December 1859, business was slowing down up north and he decided to head to London.

His train from Durham arrived late at Birmingham, missing the connection to London, so Francis had no choice but to find lodgings for the night. He trudged down to the *Crown* at Deritend to see what he could find. The landlady invited him

The Wesleyan Chapel and Crown Inn *in 1880. It was at the* Crown *that Francis fell instantly in love with Sarah.* Old and New Birmingham

into the parlour and, not long after, her daughter Sarah Pratt wandered in with the tea.

For Francis it was as though an angel had walked into the room. Her beauty instantly transfixed him. He said later it was as though she had taken possession of his soul. All thoughts of taking the train to London the next day went out of the window and he resolved to stay in Birmingham and win her heart.

It all went well to start with. He had his skills as a shoemaker and even if he didn't have the full indentures of the craft, he had his tools. By day he worked hard to get the money he needed to rent a house, and every evening he went to the pub to see Sarah. He wasn't good at making friends, everyone in the pub noticed how he only had eyes for the girl. Sarah was flattered by his

Deritend was a busy, bustling area of Birmingham, with plenty of pubs and inns to cater for the growing number of train passengers. Old and New Birmingham

attention and to a certain extent responded in kind. She agreed to marry him, although didn't go as far as setting a date.

Francis made only one friend, more of a casual acquaintance really, Police Constable Henry Evans. Evans had to put up with endless tales of how wonderful Sarah was, and little else. Evans, however, was not a little smitten with the girl himself; but he was not the kind of character who would openly tell this to Francis. He kept his intentions to himself.

In February, Sarah moved from the *Crown* to another pub, *The Swan with Two Necks*. The landlady here was Mrs Jackson, and she didn't like Francis one little bit. Another local, Mrs Thompson, seems to have taken an even more violent dislike of him. Both of them tried to persuade Sarah that Francis was no good for her. PC Evans managed to stick his oar in with a few juicy bits of gossip that made matters ten times worse. By the start of April, Mrs Jackson had fallen ill, Francis was regularly being mocked as he stood alone at the end of the bar, gazing lovingly at Sarah; and Mrs Thompson was blackening Francis with increasingly awful and untrue gossip. Unwittingly,

Francis told his apparent friend, PC Evans, about all the trouble, who promptly reported his distress back to the two old gossips.

Sarah postponed the marriage on the grounds that Mrs Jackson's illness meant she had to work harder, and then she called it off altogether, offering to give Francis his various presents back. These included a little portrait taken with the new and fashionable 'Photographic Process', at 1s 6d each. Francis was devastated. These little photographs were almost as serious as an engagement ring, each lover having a picture of the other.

He tried to work out how he could get her away from the malign influence of Mrs Thompson. PC Evans consoled him but could offer no practical help at first. On 11 April Francis had had enough of the inferring old busybody Mrs Jackson, and told Sarah that she should stop seeing her altogether, or stop seeing him. Sarah seemed very upset, even more so when

Little photographic portraits like these examples became romantic keepsakes. Sadly, although thousands survive today, few are traceable. Author's collection

Francis said that she could have her portrait back if she returned his. She went up to her room in the *Swan* and came back down with the little photograph. Wondering at the finality of the return, she refused to hand it back. Francis asked if they could make it up and she said maybe, but not until Sunday, her day off.

Francis dithered about until, on Saturday, he went back to the *Swan* to see her. Three times he was told she wasn't there, but Ellen Cain, another barmaid, told him Sarah was cleaning at an empty house not far off. Francis rushed round there to apologise and beg once more to make things up. After the most intense pleading Sarah relented and said she would see him the next day. Francis wandered off happy, so happy that he had forgotten all about the two Banbury cakes he was supposed to drop off at the *Swan*. By the time he got back there to deliver them to Mrs Thompson, Sarah had returned and gone straight up to her room in tears. Mrs Thompson told Francis this with a kind of gloating mockery.

Francis went back to the *Swan* at 11 o'clock that night. Mr and Mrs Jackson were together with Mrs Thompson. Of Sarah there was no sign. Mr Jackson started making fun of Francis about the Banbury cakes and then the pair of shoes he made for Sarah a few weeks before. Francis went home demoralised, hoping that Sarah would come to him the next day as she had promised.

Sunday came and Francis was intensely anxious, pacing up and down waiting for Sarah. By evening there was still no sign of her so he went round to the *Swan* and banged on the door. Mrs Thompson came out and told him that Sarah had been invited out by another young man, but hadn't made her mind up what to do until she knew what Francis intended. Francis told her indignantly that he intended to make it right with her and asked Mrs Thompson to go inside and tell Sarah to come out and meet him at the corner of the street. Mrs Thompson went back in, leaving Francis waiting patiently outside.

Mrs Thompson went back in and told everyone she had been talking to Francis, but she didn't know what he wanted. Ellen Cain realised this was pretty unlikely and popped out into the street. Here she met Francis and told him what had gone on. The two of them went back in to the house and Francis waited while Ellen went and fetched his portrait from the parlour. Mrs Thompson started sneering at Francis and taking the mickey out of him once again. She said if he gave her five shillings she would get Sarah to speak to him again. Mr Jackson said he could do it for half a crown. Francis went home confused, angry and deeply hurt.

Monday saw him going straight back to the *Swan* at seven in the morning. Ellen and Sarah were behind the bar getting the pub ready for the day. It was a chilly meeting. Francis pleaded with her to make it all up, but she said she would not. They shook hands very formally and Francis went back to his lodging to carry on working. Before he went it seems that he had a quiet word with Ellen in the street. Ellen hinted to him that Sarah was still really quite fond of him, and there wasn't anyone else. His emotions soared again. Back at his lodgings he found work was impossible, he was so obsessed with Sarah that he couldn't concentrate on the leather he was cutting. He tried putting a sharper edge on the sturdy clasp knife, but still nothing seemed to work right. His mind was just not on the job.

He went out and found PC Evans on his beat. Knowing that Evans knew Sarah, he begged him to set up a meeting away from the malicious Mrs Thompson. Evans said he would try to sort something out and went round to the *Swan*. He returned to tell Francis that Mrs Thompson was there so he couldn't raise the subject; Francis would just have to be patient. On the Tuesday, Evans managed to get an hour alone with Sarah and reported back to Francis that his cause was lost, there was no way he could go back to the *Swan*. Francis was mortified and urged Evans to find some way for him to talk to Sarah.

Wednesday morning came and Francis was hassling PC Evans shortly after 7 o'clock in Alcester Street. He said he would pay him five shillings to set up a meeting with Sarah. Perhaps in despair of ever getting rid of the love-sick Francis, Evans suggested that he give the money to local washerwoman Ann Home to arrange a tryst. Francis didn't waste a moment, by 7.30 am Ann Homes was on her way to the *Swan* to ask Sarah to come round to her house to meet her sister. Sarah came round, quite unaware that it was Francis who had suggested the ploy and was waiting there. Francis was in a state of nervous collapse, his mood swinging from elation that she might still love him, to the profoundest despair that he may never see her again. Had she found someone else? Were the rumours true? His mind was a whirl.

'Oh, it's you is it!' she said as Francis appeared. Ann Home decided it would be best to leave the star-crossed lovers to sort things out themselves. She left them in her front room and went out to talk to Mr Powell who was kneading up some dough in his baker's shop across the yard.

As the two chatted in the bakehouse the sound of Ann's dog growling loudly and then barking stopped their conversation. Knowing her dog wouldn't growl like that for nothing, Ann hurried across the yard and opened the door. There on the floor lay Sarah, her arm just flopping down amid a growing pool of blood. Francis pushed his way past her and ran into the yard. Ann screamed for Mr Powell to stop him.

Powell was not far behind her, he took one look at Sarah's body and set off after Francis. He managed to catch up with him by Deritend Chapel.

'What do you follow me for?' shouted Francis, turning to face him, trying to catch his breath.

'I suppose you know as well as I do.'

'I have done nothing.'

'What do you run away for then? You might as well give yourself up for you are bound to be taken.'

Francis sprinted off again and nipped around a corner into Bradford Street. Powell came round the corner to find Francis standing, still catching his breath. Luckily, John Powell's friend, Francis Stokes, arrived and the two of them overpowered Francis.

'I only gave her a smack in the mouth,' Francis protested.

'I hope it is nothing worse, but I'm afraid it is. You must go back with me and see.'

'I won't go back there, I will go to the station.'

Stokes and Powell grabbed an arm each and frogmarched him straight to the Bradford Street police station.

'Well, she shouldn't have listened to tales and then it wouldn't have happened,' moaned Francis on the way, 'I'm as bad as her, I listened to tales; well what's done can't be undone. I loved her as I love my life.'

Samuel Hobbs, the Inspector at the police station, was stunned to see Powell and Stokes dragging Francis through the door.

'What's the matter?'

'I cannot tell, but there's a woman lying down covered in blood.'

Hobbs sent a constable and then the surgeon, Mr Jordan, back to Ann Home's house. It was bad news that came back. Sarah was dead, killed almost instantly by a savage slash across her throat.

'Is she dead?' asked Francis, 'It was Mrs Jackson, Mrs Hudson and them women who was the cause of it. I shall not tell a lie about it. I loved her as I love my life. I know my fate, my days are numbered.'

Francis Price's days were indeed numbered. On 10 August, at Warwick Assizes, he was found guilty of feloniously, wilfully and maliciously murdering Sarah Pratt. A few days later he was hanged outside the gate of Warwick Gaol in front of a crowd of over a thousand jeering, voyeuristic sightseers.

CHAPTER 7

John Grayson Farquhar 1861

... a massive gunshot wound in her left breast was pouring blood and her dress was smouldering from the powder burns.

How the courts treated criminals in the nineteenth century depended to a great extent on their social standing. Paupers and the working classes had little proper legal representation, often only the clerk of the court. Occasionally, the judge would instruct a lawyer to watch over their defence, but this rarely created a level playing field. A gentleman could naturally afford the best representation, often substantially better than the crown prosecution. Not only was there this in-built inequality, but there was also a distinct tendency to try and avoid the sight of the better classes dangling on the gallows. It sent the wrong messages to a society that was supposed to believe that the upper classes were almost divinely ordained to rule wisely.

John Grayson Farquhar was a gentleman, thirty-eight years old and a man of property. As such he ran a small household in Grange Road, Small Heath; just his wife, only daughter and a couple of servants. He seems to have been well liked and respected in the locality. Unfortunately, his wife died during the 1850s, leaving him alone to raise their daughter, apart from a couple of servants of course.

In the early part of 1860 John Grayson Farquhar decided he needed a new housekeeper and so he hired the delightful Elizabeth Brookes. She was just nineteen and described as 'a girl of considerable personal attractions'. Her family came from Saltley and she often walked over there to see them.

By the New Year, their relationship had grown to something far more intimate than simply master and housekeeper. He was besotted with her and as the year wore on rumours were flying round that she would soon be Mrs Farquhar. Indeed, by mid-summer it was official, they were to be wed in the autumn. John hired another servant to take some of the domestic chores off her hands and they were often seen walking into Birmingham to go shopping.

It was after just such a trip, on 29 August 1861, that the romantic rags to riches story of Elizabeth Brookes ended. While they were in town, John Farquhar saw Elizabeth talking to a young man. He was a jealous man and the sight of her talking to this stranger rankled with him all the way through their cab drive home. He had just bought her a new dress and this was how she paid him back. The ungrateful hussy, he fumed.

When the cab brought them back to the house in Grange Road, John asked the driver in for a glass of ale. John Atkins had often brought him home and they knew each other fairly well. Standing in the parlour, John Farquhar took an old flint-lock pistol off the table and asked the cabbie if he wanted to have a shoot. Atkins declined, so John aimed the antique pistol out of the window and fired it. There was an almighty bang. Elizabeth was sitting in a chair by the garden window, probably thinking about boys and toys. She didn't speak her thoughts though.

Atkins took the pistol off the table and looked it over. It was an old type, which used a flintlock hammer to ignite the gun-powder. The hammer had three positions. After firing it lay in the little powder tray, pulling it back halfway cocked the weapon but without enough power to strike a spark and set it off. When the hammer was pulled all the way back it was at full-cock and ready to fire, assuming that the powder and shot had been loaded. John Farquhar seemed to be getting enthusiastic about his old pistol. He took a powder flask off the mantelpiece and poured a shot of powder down the barrel. The trouble was that he didn't have all the right bits for the antique gun. He rummaged in his pocket for a bit of paper to use instead of wadding, and then sent his daughter upstairs to get a tin of lead shot. When she brought it down he found the ramrod for the

Farquhar said that the pistol was accidentally triggered when Betsy put her hand on top of it. It is physically impossible for a flintlock to be triggered in this manner, so no surprise that he was found guilty. Arbour Antiques

gun was missing, and had to ram the shot down with his walking cane.

John Atkins had been in the house about fifteen minutes, and really needed to get back to work. Farquhar gave him a glass of brandy when he insisted he must get on. As Atkins turned to go Farquhar shook hands with him: 'Shake hands with me cab-man, for you will never see me any more.'

Shocked, Atkins replied: 'I shall see you many times yet, for you are a goodish sort of fellow.' Somewhat puzzled by the strange words he went back to his cab and drove off.

Quite what transpired in the parlour after Atkins left Farquhar and Elizabeth Brookes alone will never be known. After half an hour Farquhar instructed Mary Phillips, the other servant girl, to go and order another cab. Mary left the two of them alone.

A few minutes later, Mary returned with a cab, just in time to see Farquhar hurrying across the road to Mr Penny's house. She went into the house and found Elizabeth lying across two chairs, a massive gunshot wound in her left breast was pouring blood and her dress was smouldering from the powder burns. She rushed back out of the front door.

There in the street was Mr Farquhar, Mr Penny and Farquhar's little daughter playing in the road. Farquhar bent down to his daughter and said: 'I have shot Betsy.' To Mr Penny he said: 'I want you.'

Mr Penny asked what the matter was.

'Murder! By God!'

In the parlour Mr Penny found Elizabeth just as Mary had left her. The bleeding was slowing, but only because the poor girl was dying. Within minutes she had died.

'It was I shot her. It was I did the deed.'

Not surprisingly, the whole neighbourhood was alerted and Mr Degge bustled into the room. Farquhar looked at him and said: 'I have been to town to buy my housekeeper a new dress. I was doatingly fond of her. I did it and it is all through her speaking to a young man. It's through jealousy.'

A policeman arrived and Farquhar told him the same statement. He was taken to the station straight away and Inspector Hodgkins arranged to interview him. Even before Hodgkins had formally charged him, Farquhar once again admitted he had shot Elizabeth because she had been talking to a young man. Luckily for Farquhar he then shut up.

The trial in December was a sensation. All through the autumn pamphlets were going around the city dwelling on the case, everybody knew about the gentleman who shot his housekeeper, and the court was packed beyond capacity as Justice Willes sat down. The prosecution asserted that Farquhar had shot Elizabeth in a fit of jealousy. The defence claimed that she had decided to visit her family in Saltley and that Farquhar had insisted that she take a cab so that she wouldn't have the opportunity to speak to anymore young men. Playfully pointing the pistol at her to emphasise his point, she put her hand on top

The Warwickshire Advertiser *reported the case in immense detail.* Warwickshire Advertiser

WARWICKSHIRE WINTER ASSIZES.

(Before Mr. Justice WILLES.)

THE MURDER IN THE GRANGE ROAD, SMALL HEATH.

John Grayson Farquhar, 38, gentleman, was charged with the wilful murder of Elizabeth Brookes, at Small Heath, Birmingham, on the 29th of August last. He was also indicted under the coroner's inquisition, for the same offence. The prisoner pleaded "not guilty" to both indictments; he appeared to be suffering from intense anguish of mind, and was allowed to be seated in a chair at the bar during the trial.—Mr. Adams, with Mr. Palmer (instructed by Mr. A. Walter, of this town) appeared for the prosecution; and Mr. Macaulay, Q.C., and Mr. O'Brien (instructed by Mr. J. Powell) defended the prisoner. The court and its approaches were crowded to excess with persons from Birmingham and the neighbourhood, to whom the prisoner had been well known for years.

The massive bore of an old flintlock pistol shows just how deadly a weapon it could be. Arbour Antiques

of the barrel and inadvertently knocked the flintlock, setting off the powder. He hadn't realised that when he put the pistol down on the table after talking with Atkins, it was at full-cock, not half. Just a slight brush of the hand was enough to fire the gun, and he couldn't tell whether it was his or her hand that had triggered the vicious antique.

The judge discounted all the statements Farquhar made indicating his guilt since they were made before he was properly charged. A drawing made to indicate how Elizabeth must have been sitting down when she was shot was also disallowed on the ground that it might unduly excite the jury. The jury were instructed to bear in mind that there was no real motive for murder, and if the gunshot was accidental then the charge must be manslaughter not murder. They retired for a short while and came back with the verdict of guilty of manslaughter, but with no recommendation for mercy. Justice Willes condemned Farquhar to life imprisonment, the most severe punishment he could.

Who knows what happened in that little parlour in Grange Road? Farquhar was jealous certainly, but not in a violent rage

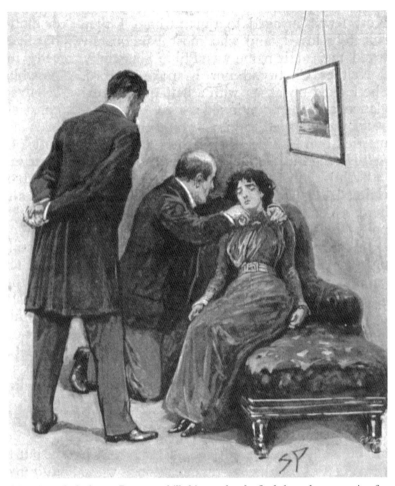

Shot through the heart, Betsy was killed instantly, the flash from the gun setting fire to her dress. Strand Magazine

when the cabman left. Perhaps Farquhar was simply an idiot for leaving a loaded and cocked gun on the table. He was in a state of nervous collapse at the trial, unable to stand at the dock. His admissions of guilt would have ensured a speedy execution if he had not been a gentleman, but life imprisonment in Victorian times was as much a death sentence as if he had been sent straight to the gallows.

CHAPTER 8

The Tranter Street Murder 1861

... Ann Walker had bled to death from two massive gashes across her throat ...

Life had not been particularly kind to John Thompson. By the time he was forty-two, in 1861, he was left a widower with five hungry children. Thompson was a skilled wiredrawer by trade, working at a factory in Aston and living in a house in Sutton Coldfield. He was considered a respectable and hard working member of the community. The house that he lived in was built by the local authority, one of the 'Corporation houses'. He was allowed to live in it rent free; such was his reputation as a serious and steady man. No one had any idea of the storm in his life that was to follow. As is often the case in these circumstances, he had to hire a housekeeper to look after his children. In May 1860, he found Ann Walker. She was in urgent need of a roof over her head and soon filled the role of 'housekeeper'. Their relationship rapidly became an intimate one but John Thompson was not fully aware of Ann's past life.

Ann Walker was married for one thing. She had been married for many years to a well-to-do mechanic, but for some reason she started drinking heavily and eventually turned to prostitution to pay for her habit. Disgusted, her husband gave up on her and moved to Manchester to work as a glassblower. Ann spent a fair while drifting from man to man around Birmingham, a slave of the booze, exploited by all and sundry. She was a regular at Emma Beresford's brothel in Tranter Street. John Thompson was unaware that she also went by the names Ann Lines and Nancy Dawson.

Perhaps things started to look up when she moved in with John Thompson. She had a regular diet and the duties and

The Bull Ring was always busy, but during the annual fair the whole city was packed with people from the surrounding countryside. Old and New Birmingham

discipline of running a household with five children. It was not to last though. John himself quite liked a drop of the hard stuff and seems to have had a fiery temper as well. Ann's past was not going to vanish that quickly.

On Saturday 28 September the two of them went into Birmingham for the annual fair. As was common for the Birmingham Fair, they spent the day drinking and larking about. Pretty drunk by the evening, they staggered into the Tranter Street brothel and Ann persuaded Emma Beresford to give them a room for the night. The following morning they carried on with the marathon drinking session.

Ann and John gradually worked their way round the pubs until they got to *The Engine House* at Dale End in the mid-afternoon. John left her alone in the bar for a few minutes and when he returned he found her in deep and very familiar conversation with one of her former lovers. John Thompson blew his top and furiously stormed out of the pub. Ann stayed on a bit longer and then wove her unsteady way back to the

The centre of Birmingham was packed with run-down alleys and courts, home to brothels and drinking dens – like Tranter Street which was demolished to clean-up the area. Old and New Birmingham

Tranter Street brothel where she staggered upstairs to sleep it off. John Thompson got back there a few minutes afterwards and made his way upstairs too. For a few tense minutes the house was quiet.

A shriek of 'Murder!' roused Emma Beresford and one of the girls called Green. They ran up to the attic, barged open the door and found John Thompson lying on top of Ann Walker, cutting her throat with a clasp knife. Emma called out of a window for help and a man called Careless raced up the stairs to intervene. By the time he got to the attic, Ann Walker had bled to death from two massive gashes across her throat, right from ear to ear, deluging the floor with blood. Careless collared a seemingly bemused Thompson and asked: 'What did you do it for?' Thompson just shrugged and casually said: 'I have done it.' Careless prised the clasp knife from his left hand and held onto him until PC Copestake arrived and handcuffed the still dazed Thompson. When Copestake told him he would be charged with murder he again shrugged and just said: 'Alright.'

John Thompson faced trial immediately after John Grayson Farquhar. He had no defence counsel and was thus given Mr O'Brien to plead his case. The prosecution case was pretty much watertight, and O'Brien could only suggest that in the few moments that the pair of them were alone in the room, before the cries of murder, that they had had a row, and then a fight, and then the stabbing took place. John Thompson was not in his right mind because of the amount of alcohol he had consumed over the previous forty-eight hours. It was not a premeditated act and so should be manslaughter not murder. He begged the jury to show the degree of justice as they would to someone in a higher walk of life. It was a distinct allusion to the previous case where Farquhar had shot his housekeeper/ lover at point blank range and been spared the gallows. The year 1861 was not proving to be a good one for housekeepers.

The jury weren't of the same opinion, Thompson was found guilty, and Justice Willes had clearly had enough of drink-related crimes, after a stern sermon about the evils of drink he put on his black cap and condemned John Thompson to death for his crime. Thompson took the grim sentence with apparent indifference and walked from the court with a steady step towards his doom.

There was widespread disquiet at the sentence. Thompson's case seemed so similar to that of Farquhar to the general public that everyone started muttering that the justice administered depended on your station in life; Farquhar the gentleman was imprisoned but Thompson the labourer was sent to the gallows. A memorial was sent to the Home Secretary pleading for Thompson's death sentence to be commuted. This was signed by many of the local magistrates and lawyers, the local gentry and even the Mayor of Birmingham. It read:

The memorial of the undersigned inhabitants of Birmingham respectfully showeth, -1- that John Thompson, labourer, was convicted of murder and sentenced to be hanged at the recent

Winter Assizes for the county of Warwick upon evidence that showed he was under the combined influence of drunkenness and jealousy at the time when the murder was committed. That in these respects the case bore a striking similarity to the cases of John Grayson Farquhar, gentleman, who was convicted at the same assizes of the crime of manslaughter and sentenced to penal servitude for life. That your memorialists fear that the execution of Thompson will seriously prejudice the solemn interests of public justice in this town and neighbourhood, as the two cases have generally been considered of similar character, and it is most deeply to be regretted that a painful feeling of uncertainty respecting the administration of the law should be allowed to creep into the public mind. That your memorialists earnestly entreat that you will take the whole of the facts into your consideration with a view to the commutation of the sentence of death.

It was to be of no avail, the Home Secretary saw no reason to interfere with the judicial process and on 3 January three prisoners appeared at the gates of Warwick Gaol for a brief church service. John Grayson Farquhar was going to prison for the rest of his life, sobbing and moaning all through the service before being escorted away to prison. John Thompson together with William Beamish were marched to the gallows. Beamish was to hang for poisoning his wife and children with arsenic in an attempt to clear a path for him to marry his girlfriend. He was a pretty nasty piece of work, pleading that he didn't mean to poison his little daughter, but instead of going to her funeral he went out and celebrated with his fancy woman, Emma Stratham. Still, Beamish came from Coventry and Stratham from Warwick, so their tawdry and tragic tale needn't worry us here.

At 9.48, the turnkeys stood the doomed men on the trapdoor, George Smith Dudley put linen bags over their heads, arranged the nooses and quickly walked back down the scaffold steps and withdrew the bolt. The two men dropped before the crowd even realised the time had come. Those who saw the dreadful deed suddenly drew a breath and, for a moment, silence fell across the assembly.

CHAPTER 9

An Odd Year
1861

As a highwayman he was a bit of a dead loss really.

A book about murders does rather tend to be unremittingly grim, both researching and writing it. One does develop a rather cavalier and callous attitude to human frailty, the heart tends to sink at the thought of yet another person saving the cost of a divorce lawyer by cutting his wife's throat, and wish they could be at least a little more imaginative in their choice of weapon. Cut-throat razors weren't named that way because they just looked threatening; they had a top notch track record too. However, the crime pages of the Victorian era do raise a wry chuckle from time to time, if only at the bizarre range of cases the assizes had to deal with.

The date 3 August 1861 is pretty typical. There weren't any sensational cases, no one looked certain to get sent to the gallows, but there was always the off chance that the Justice was in a filthy mood and the court was packed with people. This was long before television and some cases were as sensational as any soap opera today.

First up was Sarah Pratt, aged twenty-three. She had stabbed Sarah Anne Ellwood because she had started walking out with her ex-boyfriend, William Haden. Quite what really happened outside Saltley College will never be known. Sarah Pratt swears that William had assaulted her in a brutal manner and she had drawn the knife in self-defence and accidentally stabbed her rival. Sarah Ellwood swore that Miss Pratt stabbed her in the shoulder and ran off shouting she wished she had killed both of them. Mr Solomon Charles Smith, the surgeon at Birmingham General Hospital looked at the wound and dismissed it as

Digbeth was a seething mass of humanity. In the backstreets, all manner of villains lurked, waiting for some unsuspecting gentleman to wander past. Old and New Birmingham

scarcely deeper than the skin. Sarah Pratt was sentenced to one week's imprisonment for that little fracas.

The next case was a bit more gory, once again it involved a knife, but this time it was a proper Saturday night bar room brawl, albeit with tragic consequences. Samuel Bostock and Duke Mitchinson were drinking in the *Black Lion* in Coleshill Street. Also in the bar were John Ridley and Walter Barber. It was about 11.00 pm and no doubt everyone was a bit worse for wear. Bostock and Barber started calling each other names and generally getting aggressive. Mitchinson went and whispered something to Bostock, then smacked him in the mouth. Bostock reeled back and Mitchinson, a very powerfully-built man, hit him again. Bostock yelled at him: 'Stand off, or I will give you something you will carry for life.'

Mitchinson was not easily frightened and rushed at Bostock. The force of the charge carried the pair of them into the passage and then Bostock managed to wriggle free and run into the yard. Mitchinson caught him there and grabbed him by the hair, repeatedly hitting in the face. As John Ridley ran out to calm things down both men had collapsed to the floor. 'Be quiet', called Ridley and managed to cool them off a bit.

'Oh, I have kinked my back,' said Mitchinson, 'feel what a lump there is.'

Ridley checked and found a large swelling with blood oozing out of it. Some friends carried him off to the General Hospital. James Langford spotted a knife in a water tub; there was fresh blood on it. By now Samuel Copestake, one of the few police in the city had arrived and he arrested Bostock. Samuel Bostock told him: 'I should not have done it if he had not struck me first.'

The surgeon, Mr Alfred Baker, sewed up the wounds in Mitchinson's back and for about a day he looked as though he would be alright. This was 1861, there were no antibiotics or neat ways to stitch up a perforated bowel. The following day he developed a widespread infection and on 22 July he died.

The jury found Bostock guilty of manslaughter and, taking the circumstances of the fight into account, sentenced him to six months' imprisonment with hard labour.

Duke Mitchinson was just one of thousands who sought help at the General Hospital, but in an era before anaesthetics and antibiotics, there was little that the surgeons could do to help him. Old and New Birmingham

Warwick Assizes were living up to their reputation of lots of interesting dramas. Next was the case of Isaac Allsop, twenty-nine, charged with highway robbery with violence. As a highwayman he was a bit of a dead loss really. On the night of 1 May, William Cheshire was walking down Aston Road when Allsop stopped him and asked if he could buy him a drink. William Cheshire must have been in a generous mood because he took this complete stranger at face value. The two of them went into the *Castle* and had a couple of gins. When they came back out into the street Allsop repaid William's generosity by grabbing him and throwing him to ground. Allsop ripped his watch from his pocket and ran off towards Pritchett Street. William managed to get up and chase him. Allsop rounded the corner into Pritchett Street and ran straight into the arms of a policeman. He got ten months' imprisonment with hard labour for that little escapade.

John Burke was the next man in the dock. He was accused of having struck William Hayes on the head with a spade, twice. It seems to have been a family feud, John Burke had pushed his way into Hayes' house on the evening of 6 May. When William came in he was having a fight with his brother, Henry Hayes. William managed to grab him and then wrestle him out of the front door. This wasn't the end of the matter at all. Burke returned with his brother-in-law very quickly and tried to force his way back in. Despite William's best efforts, the front door gave way and Burke burst in and cracked him on the head with the edge of the spade, leaving two ragged wounds right down to the bone. Park Lane wasn't a peaceful suburb in those days. Burke was sentenced to nine months with hard labour.

There were a few burglaries for the court to hear. The first was caught when the gang tried to pawn the clothes that they had stolen. The second burglary was foiled before anything was stolen. Mr Brown, who lived at the *Old Union Mill Inn* heard a noise in the middle of the night and armed himself with a cutlass before venturing downstairs. He clearly put the fear of God into James Davis and Andrew Hennam, who fled as fast as they could. Henman jumped into the canal in a bid to avoid capture by the enraged, sword-wielding Mr Brown. Brown managed to catch Davis, and the local police caught Hennam the next morning, his clothes still soaking from his dip in the cut. Davis got five years and Hennam was sentenced to seven since he already had a long criminal record.

Not all crimes were so straightforward. Sarah Ransford accused Rupert Riley of raping her, but had no way of proving that it was him since there were no witnesses. Her case collapsed.

The punishments meted out at the Assizes were anything but consistent. Sarah Patrick was not on the best of terms with her brother-in-law Edwin Patrick, but they did manage to go out to *Clement's Liquor Vault* in Newton Row on the evening of Saturday 11 May. As they came out, Edwin's so called 'girl friend', Elisa Roberts, came up to them and grabbed the cap off his head and ran away. He chased and caught up with her by Bassett's greengrocers. She wouldn't give the cap back to him, and Sarah, who was just behind them, shouted: 'Don't give it to the b**** thief.' Edwin turned and shook his fist in her face. At this threat she pulled the cork off a bottle of 'Smoking Salts', a vicious chemical used in her job as a metal solderer, and flung the contents in his face. 'Come on Lis, I have blinded the b****.' The flux went straight into his eyes. The two girls ran off leaving him screaming in agony, completely blind. Edwin Patrick was horribly burned and had to spend three weeks in the General Hospital before he could see again. Despite all the pain, during the court case he asked the judge to deal mercifully with Sarah, and as a result she was discharged once she promised never to do anything of the kind again.

The following day, the inconsistency of sentences is once again apparent. Despite the vast number of factories and work-shops springing up on every vacant spot of land around the district, there was still a hint of the countryside in the air. George Gibbs, a nineteen-year-old labourer, was sentenced to eight months for committing an unnatural offence with a mare. Another labourer, Edward Collins, was sentenced to eighteen months for exactly the same offence. There may be some details missing that would explain the difference, but given the nature of the charge, do we really want to know them? No. Joseph Boyes managed to get acquitted on his charge of an unnatural offence with a lamb in a field near Coventry. Poor little thing!

Most of the crimes that were tried at Warwick related to Birmingham. The sheer number of people living there made

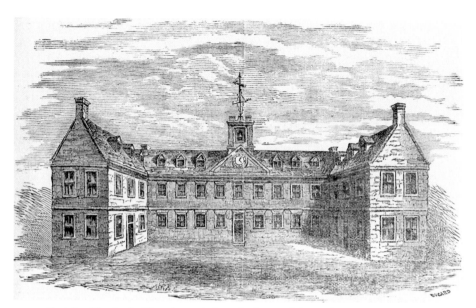

Social welfare in the Victorian period revolved around the workhouse. Some paupers were given cash to help them remain independent; those too elderly or too weak to fend for themselves were housed in the workhouse. It was not a pleasant option. Old and New Birmingham

sure of that. Birmingham itself was only made a borough in 1838 and relied on an old lock-up and a handful of policemen. Provision for the poor was no longer just a matter of locking them up in the workhouse but giving them a small amount of money as dole. It didn't take long for someone to spot a weakness in the system and exploit it.

Also in court that year was Henry James Smith, the relieving officer responsible for investigating and distributing parish relief in District 3. A pauper could apply to him for aid and he would enter their details in the register and issue a pass ticket. This ticket was then presented once a week at the pay-desk and the clerk, Edward Rutherford, would hand over the relief money. Half-a-crown a week was not really enough to live on, but then there were thousands in need and that was as much as the guardians of the poor of the parish of Birmingham could raise on the parish rate. The ticket was destroyed when the claimant died or no longer needed the relief.

Pay-day was usually mayhem, 600–700 people descended on the Union for their dole. A good proportion of them collected money for elderly and infirm relatives as well as their own, which meant it was difficult to spot any frauds in progress. It left Henry James Smith in a position to make a little on the side. All he had to do was to forget to remove someone who had died from the register and then get someone else to use the ticket to collect the cash.

The winter of 1860/61 was hard enough to see off quite a few elderly paupers, Ann Piddy died on 2 January, Mr Newman on the 10th and no doubt there were many more. Henry Smith did not strike their entries from the register, but asked Mary Farrell to collect their dole for them, and give it to him so that he could take it around personally. How very charitable of him. She was already collecting relief for her mother and thought she was helping other elderly people even though she didn't know who they were. Smith thought he was on to a nice little earner. This dubious state of affairs lasted until July. By then knowledge of the deaths of Ann Piddy and Mr Newman reached the ears of other relieving officers.

PC Frederick Kelly confiscated the two pass tickets from Mary Farrell and then arrested Henry Smith. An examination of the books didn't show up any other cases, so this wasn't a widespread fraud; just one corrupt official. Justice Willes gave him a ferocious lecture about the duties of public service and then sentenced him to six months' hard labour.

CHAPTER 10

Henry Carter
1863

Henry Carter was completely besotted with Alice ...

Jealousy and revenge are two recurring themes within this book. Some people just won't take no for an answer and get decidedly bitter and twisted when their desires are thwarted. Henry Carter was a keen churchgoer, but even that was not enough to conquer the green-eyed demon.

Henry Carter was a lightly built young man of twenty. He had a fair coloured skin and light brown hair. He worked as a brass founder at Messrs Whitehouse & Sons, Birchalls Street, in 1862. A reliable and industrious character, he was a regular attendant at the Circus Chapel Sunday School in Bradford Street. In April of that year he spotted a pretty young girl coming out of a house on his way to work. It wasn't long before he introduced himself to her.

The Warwickshire Advertiser *covered the sensational case in great detail.*
Warwickshire Advertiser

Warwickshire Lent Assizes.
(CONCLUDED FROM LAST WEEK'S PAPER.)

CROWN COURT—SATURDAY.
(Before Mr. JUSTICE WILLES.) .

THE MURDER OF ALICE HINKLEY, AT BIRMINGHAM.

The Court opened at nine o'clock this morning, when *Henry Carter* was placed in the dock, and arraigned for the wilful murder of Alice Hinkley, at Birmingham, on the 4th of December last. The prisoner, on entering the dock, was accommodated with a chair, which he used from time to time during the trial. His appearance—a figure slight for 20 years of age, fair complexion, and hair of a light brown hue, evidently excited much compassion. Considerable interest was manifested in the case, several ladies were present, and admission was confined to holders of tickets in order to prevent the Court from being inconveniently crowded.

Alice Hinkley lived with her parents and grandparents in part of Orton's Buildings, in a court off Bissell Street. Henry Carter was completely besotted with Alice and came round to her house to formally ask her father if he could 'walk out' with her. Although her father had no objection, Alice wasn't overly enamoured of Henry and kept herself quite aloof. Henry came round to her house virtually every day after work and, on Sundays, would treat her to an outing to a church where there was a good sermon – not perhaps the most exciting courtship on offer even in those days. It wasn't long before they had exchanged little photographic portraits of each other, as much a sign of intentions as an engagement ring; although Alice might not have been whisked off her feet by his charm. Henry was a good solid worker and would be able to earn the money to set her up in a good household. Her parents bore this in mind just as much as Henry's ardour.

Spring turned to summer and Alice was growing increasingly tired of Henry's fawning attentions. By mid-summer she broke off their relationship, but with no one else in sight, and her parents' pressure, took Henry back. They broke up once again during the autumn, but drifted back together by November. Even if the match with Henry met with her parents' approval, it didn't stop Alice keeping an eye open for someone less claustrophobically affectionate and it seems that towards the end of November she had found a person who was a good deal more fun than Henry. As this new acquaintance paid her more attention, so she paid less interest to poor old Henry. He was having enough trouble anyway; he had lost his job at Whitehouse & Sons and was frantically looking for work, without a good job his last chance of persuading Alice's father to let him marry her was fading fast.

Henry knew there was someone else and was getting furiously jealous, even though his nightly visits to Alice's family house were amicable enough. In the first days of December he was publicly humiliated in the street by this other suitor, the man spat in his face and called him for everything. Jealousy, resentment and impotent rage all seethed within his apparently Christian heart. Turning the other cheek seemed to lose its appeal.

A double-barrelled pistol of the type used by Carter. It had a large bore and used percussion caps to detonate the powder in each barrel. At close quarters it was a formidable weapon. Arbour Antiques

On the afternoon of 4 December, Samuel Moore, a friend and neighbour of Carter bumped into him by the pawnbrokers in Smallbrook Street. Samuel asked him if he was looking for a watch.

'No, I'm looking for a pistol,' Carter replied.

Samuel jokingly asked if he wanted to shoot himself, but Henry said it was for a friend in the country. The two of them walked along to Wesman Street and found a gun shop there. They looked over the range and Carter bought a rather cheap double-barrelled pistol, some gunpowder and percussion caps. The pistol might have had a cheap cocking mechanism, but the barrels were rifled for the latest style of bullet. The gun shop

These pistols had to be loaded with powder and shot each time they were fired. Arbour Antiques

The Minié style of bullet was conical, enabling the new type of rifled barrel to spin the bullet, making it far more accurate. The hollow end ensured a better fit in the barrel and so it was a much more powerful projectile. Alice Hinkley died almost instantly.
Arbour Antiques

had no bullets of the right calibre in stock. The two men wandered off to the nearest pub for a drink, and then off to another pub for another, they probably weren't too popular because they were playing with the pistol, firing the percussion caps at the gas mantles.

Henry and Samuel finally went round to Mr Henry Hart's gun shop in Pershore Street.

'I want three penny-worth of bullets for this pistol,' said Henry.

Mr Hart looked at the double-barrelled pistol; he was a bit dubious about the calibre and hunted through a bowl of round bullets to see if there was anything the right size. Samuel Moore spotted a glass case full of the latest style, the Minié bullet. These were a conical shape rather than the normal sphere. They had to be fired from a rifled barrel.

'They would go through a man,' Hart, the shop-owner observed.

'Would they?', Carter asked.

'Wouldn't they?', Moore asked Mr Hart.

Hart told them how a soldier had shot his officer with one of these and the bullet had gone right through him and killed the man behind him.

Carter bought two.

Mr Hart told Carter to be very careful with the pistols; they would go a long way. Carter and Moore left with the two lethal projectiles as well as a bag of ordinary round bullets. Moore left Carter at his uncle's house in Branstone Street at about 7 o'clock.

Moore didn't notice anything unusual about Henry Carter that afternoon. They had been to a few pubs, looked in a few shop windows, had fun blowing the gas mantles off their jets with the pistol, nothing particularly sinister worried Samuel as he said goodbye to Henry.

Henry Carter made his usual visit to Alice Hinkley at her father's house a bit after 8 o'clock that evening. They chatted away, apparently happy enough until 10.30 pm when it was time for Henry to go home and Alice to return to her lodgings. Outside, they stood in the entry to the court, still talking normally enough. Alice's granny, Elizabeth Hinkley passed then as she went to visit a neighbour. She told Alice not to hang about in the cold.

Marie Cowrie came past and saw Alice, saying: 'How foolish you are to stand there with such a cold as you've got.'

'I haven't been here more than half a minute,' replied Alice.

Marie turned to go. As she left she heard Carter say to Alice: 'Do you mean it?'

'Yes!' she replied.

Marie Cowrie had walked only twenty paces when she heard an almighty bang. At first she thought it was from the factory at the bottom of the yard. As she turned around Carter sprinted past her. Not realising anything was amiss, she carried on with her errand to fetch some beer.

Elizabeth Hinkley heard the shot from the neighbour's house and rushed out to see what was wrong. Her granddaughter was lying on the ground at the entrance to the court. She was already dead. She got help to drag the poor girl into her house. Alice Hinkley had a single gunshot wound in her back. The alarm was raised, a surgeon called, but Carter had disappeared into the night.

Mr Warrilow, the surgeon, arrived to examine Alice. PC McCauseland was sent out to search for Carter. For over an hour he tramped the dark streets without any result until he heard the distant sound of voices from Bissell Street. He sprinted back to Orton Buildings to find a throng of people about the door of the Hinkleys.

'Here he is!' they were shouting.

He pushed and shoved his way to the front of the crowd to find none other than Henry Carter frantically trying to batter his way into the house shouting: 'I must see her. I will see her,' despite the dozens of people attempting to stop him.

Carter struggled with demented strength. Sergeant Jarvis had to help McCauseland restrain him and drag him off towards the Bradford Street police station. On the way Jarvis heard something drop to the pavement. It was the pistol.

'You've dropped this,' Jarvis said to Carter.

'I was about to give it to you,' replied Carter.

Superintendent Sullivan inspected the gun closely at the station. One barrel had been fired. Fortunately he had the good sense to call for Mr Hart. The other barrel had been loaded with a simply insane amount of gunpowder. If it had been fired the entire gun would have exploded. The officer also found one little photographic portrait in his pocket. It was the one of Carter that Alice must have given him back that evening. It was a tangible reminder to him that their relationship was at an end and quite probably the final straw that tipped him into a homicidal rage.

Mr Warrilow made a more detailed post-mortem examination the following day. Alice must have turned her back on Henry Carter after handing him the little photograph and at that moment he pulled the gun out of his pocket and fired it upwards from waist height. The Minié bullet struck her between shoulder blade and spine, shattering her 5th rib, passing through one of the major arteries and ending up inside her neck. She died within a few seconds of such a massive injury. The bullet was none other than one of the pair that Carter bought from Mr Hart.

Henry Carter was tried at Warwick Assizes on 3 April 1863. Not surprisingly he was found guilty. His defence tried to allege that the gun could have gone off accidentally, but no one was convinced. A death sentence was inevitable in these circumstances.

In spite of the clear evidence of his guilt many people found the sentence of death unduly harsh and distasteful. There was a general feeling that Alice had treated him pretty harshly, strung him along and exploited his youthful naivety. He was driven to distraction by her infidelity and he must have been temporarily insane when he resolved to shoot her. Henry Carter was a broken and utterly contrite man now, praying to God for forgiveness and writing abject letters of apology to Alice's parents and friends.

Some of the leading lawyers and civic dignitaries of Birmingham raised a petition to the Home Secretary to have the sentence commuted to life imprisonment. They had to work quickly too. The law was that at least two Sundays must pass between sentence of death and execution, beyond this was at the discretion of the Sheriff of Warwick. This Sheriff was not known for letting things drag on. Henry was sentenced on 3 April, and the execution was set for Monday 11 April. The petition was at first sent and then another telegraphed to Sir George Gray, the Home Secretary, but received no response.

Over the weekend before the dreaded date, a deputation tried to contact Sir George Gray in person, but they missed him at his office as he had just left for Windsor Castle; and they missed him there on the Saturday as he had returned to London to respond to another petition from the Unitarian Minister at Warwick. The deputation raced back to Whitehall to find that they had missed him once again. There was a letter for them.

The Home Secretary saw no reason to interfere with the proper decision of the judge.

Henry Carter died on the scaffold just after 10 o'clock on Monday 11 April 1863. A crowd of around a thousand had come down from Birmingham on the train and watched in grim silence. Henry gave a short speech encouraging others to learn from his example, and died instantly of a broken neck.

A short while after his body was cut down there was a knock on the gates of the gaol. An old lady from Tachbrook stood there with her daughter. The daughter had a large tumour growing on her neck and in true traditional style the old lady asked if the executed man's hand could be drawn across it to affect a cure. The warders refused such an absurd request and slammed the gate in her face. Times were indeed changing.

CHAPTER 11

The Castle Street Murder 1888

George suddenly pulled out the revolver ...

Mental illness can be readily diagnosed these days, but in the Victorian era matters were far less clear. Mood swings and hyperactive behaviour were clearly recognised but some of their consequences were misunderstood. There was no effective treatment in any case, so perhaps the tragedy of the Castle Street Murder was inevitable.

George Nathaniel Daniels was prone to mood swings and tended to get wildly over excited about the smallest things. He was born in 1859 to a large Worcestershire family. In due course he married and was soon the father of a girl and a boy. He was considered to be both a good father and dutiful son. However, there was a certain mental weakness that seemed to run in the family. In 1873, his uncle tried to kill himself, leaping through his bedroom window and running off across the fields to fling himself in a pond. He made a similar attempt a year later. George's own father attempted to throw himself off the River Severn bridge at Worcester and had to be physically restrained. Life was not to get any kinder to George; his wife died, leaving him with two children to rear alone.

George managed to get the children lodged with Jane Edmonds, at Upper Woodings Farm, Bromyard while he came to Birmingham to earn enough money to pay for their keep. George managed to get a job as a printer's porter at Britten's Printers, 78 High Street, in 1885. He managed to find lodgings at 25 Conybeare Street and at first all seemed to go well. He suffered from headaches from time to time, but no one he worked or lodged with thought that there was anything particularly odd about him.

ASTON CHURCH & PARK ENTRANCE

The area around Aston had its scenic attractions as well as a bloodthirsty history.
Author's collection

In August 1887, he met Emma Elizabeth Hastings who was the daughter of the family that ran the *Golden Elephant* in Castle Street. A passionate romance soon overwhelmed both of them. George came round to the pub every single evening, occasionally coming to dinner as well. Mr and Mrs Hastings thought he was quite a pleasant young man, and probably a good match for Emma. Every time George went to visit his children in Bromyard the two of them sent letters to each other every day. Certainly for George this was an all embracing infatuation that overwhelmed him. His letters seem to have been mawkishly sentimental and, of course, they had exchanged photographs. Emma seems to have been just as smitten with him.

George's mood swings had brought him near to ruin in the year before he met Emma. He had sought excitement and distraction by betting on the horses and, as is so often the case, it virtually bankrupted him. He drank to console himself. Not a good combination at all. By the time they were going steady together he was trying to pick himself up again. In one letter to his beloved 'Pem' he wrote: 'All that rings in my head is ruin. Oh Pem, if I had known you twelve months ago I would never have done it all.'

One of her letters sent him tumbling in a spiral of despair. It read:

My dear, no doubt you will be angry with me with what I am going to say but I can't help it. Since Tuesday night it has come into my head that you did not love me. My God, what should I do if it were. Dear, excuse me saying that, but it is from the depth of my aching heart; it does go as it never did before.

It took very little to plunge George even further into a black mood. One of his letters went:

You walk about and treat me with contempt as though you did not care for me. I have told you several times I am poor, but I may in time be once again what I have been. You never in your life put me about so much as you did last night. I cannot sleep nor rest to do anything . . . Never let my name trouble you; let it leave your mind as though I was dead, for I am sure I wish I was. Oh Pem, I never thought you would do such a thing as you did last night. So goodbye, if not for ever, for I could never pass you by, oh, never. Pem, good-bye, God Bless you . . .

By 1888 the English-style revolver was in common use. The cylinder contained six sections in which powder and shot were loaded, each being fired by a percussion cap. The increased power from the rifle barrel and conical bullets allowed a smaller bore to be used with just as much lethal force as the older, single-barrelled guns. Arbour Antiques

The rest of the letter is a rambling incoherent monologue of self-pity accusing her of breaking his heart. If Emma hadn't been so besotted with him, she would probably have taken the letter as a warning that he was becoming dangerously unstable.

February 1888 saw George drinking harder. His workmates noticed how his usual jocular character was changing. He gradually became more taciturn and morose. He kept on seeing his beloved Pem each night; he was pretty much part of the family by now. Some deep change had occurred inside his love-addled and unstable mind. On 31 March he bought a revolver from the pawnbrokers in the High Street, ostensibly to have some sport during a visit to the country. To give him the benefit of the doubt it must be said that he had promised Jane Edmonds that he would bring her something to scare the crows off the wheat on her farm. Mind you, a revolver is hardly the ideal tool for the job.

Quite what he had in mind remains a mystery. On the afternoon of 14 April he went into the bar of *Bullivant's Hotel* in the High Street. He seemed in a cheerful enough mood. He was chatting with Frederick Rainbow, the baker. Fred joked with him about the very pretty girl he had seen him with the day before. George replied: 'She'll look much nicer when she has this through her!' and pulled out the revolver.

A stunned silence fell over the bar. Fred, Alfred Bowler and the barmaid, Miss Musto, didn't know what to say. George left, still smiling, and muttering: 'I wish I was dead.'

Something was deeply wrong.

George Daniels turned up at the *Golden Elephant* that evening as usual. He and Emma went into the sitting room and stayed there chatting whilst Mrs Hastings went out. Mr Hastings was serving in the bar. Mrs Hastings came back to the pub at 11 o'clock, closing time, when Mr Hastings was ushering the last few customers out into the night. George was standing by the door of the sitting room and Mrs Hastings asked him what the time was. He answered her perfectly normally. Emma had just gone to the kitchen. Mrs Hastings popped out for a minute to see her neighbour, Mrs Vernon.

Emma's sister, Alice Louise, was sitting in the kitchen alone when Emma came in. Emma picked up a comb and started plaiting her fourteen-year-old sister's long hair. She was sitting on the edge of the sink. George came into the kitchen, walked over to Emma and kissed her on the cheek. He asked Emma to go with him to the door.

'Wait till I've finished my sister's hair,' she replied.

George walked over to the fireplace and stood there with his back to the flames. A minute or so passed in silence. George suddenly pulled out the revolver and shot Emma. She fell to the floor.

Alice Louise shrieked and bolted out of the door. As she fled she heard a second shot.

Mrs Hastings was just coming back down the hall when Alice burst out of the kitchen, screaming. With Mrs Vernon close behind she raced to see what the matter was. Emma was sitting on the floor between the sink and the dresser, bleeding from a wound in her temple. George was still standing by the fireplace, the revolver in his hand. He didn't say a word.

Mrs Vernon ran out into the street to find a cab to get Emma to the hospital. The gunshots had roused half the neighbourhood and people were hurrying towards the pub. Mr Hastings got back and entered the kitchen; on seeing Emma on the floor he passed out from the shock. Several men rushed into the pub to find George still there, dazed and confused. He had sat down with his head in his hands. Mr Pearce and Herbert King restrained him, and took the gun from his pocket. PC Samuel Wellings soon arrived, quickly followed by PC George Nicholls. They took the gun off Pearce and examined it. Three of the chambers were empty, and of the three that held charges two had been recently fired. They wondered if George was saving the last for himself.

Emma was rushed to the General Hospital. Mr Elliott, the surgeon on duty, found she had one bullet lodged in her left breast, which he managed to extract without difficulty. There was another gunshot wound to her temple, but fired at much closer range. Around the puncture was a speckling of powder burns. Again he managed to get the bullet out, but the wound was deeper and far more serious. It seems that the first shot had knocked Emma to the ground and then, as Alice fled screaming from the sudden horror, George had walked over to Emma and deliberately shot her in the head.

George was locked up in Moor Street police station. Emma regained consciousness the following day and a magistrate went to interview her. There was widespread confusion about why George had suddenly changed from a devoted lover to a homicidal maniac. George himself seemed just as confused; unable to remember anything of the events from before he went into *Bullivant's Hotel* until he woke in Moor Street police cell.

Emma Hastings refused to make any statement to the magistrate, despite repeated pleas from the surgeon as well. As the days passed, she grew steadily more ill, an infection set into her head wound and on 20 April she died.

A distraught George Daniels was now charged with wilful murder. He had begged and pleaded to be allowed to see his beloved Pem whilst she was in hospital, but it was not allowed. He wrote letters to her parents afterwards attempting to obtain their forgiveness, with little effect. He was finally brought to trial on 3 August. There was much argument as to his state of mind. Had he been seized by some momentary madness? The killing was so unexpected that it simply didn't fit anyone's frame of reference. There was no other lover to drive him to a fit of jealousy, no sudden and abrupt end to the courtship. It just

By 1888, Birmingham had its own law courts and assizes. Author's collection

didn't make sense. The bundle of letters that George had kept showed he was a rather unstable character, and his pitiful outbursts of tears in the courtroom reinforced the opinion that he was a bit weak in the head. However, the purchase of the revolver a fortnight before the incident seemed to indicate a plan and malice that meant it was no sudden impulse but a callously premeditated killing.

The jury took just ten minutes to find George Nathaniel Daniels guilty of wilful murder. He went to the gallows on 28 August, hanged alongside Harry Jones inside Winson Green Prison.

CHAPTER 12

Harry Jones
1888

Harry decided to kill them all ...

Harry Jones, who met our previous villain very briefly on the scaffold, was a very different character indeed. He was only twenty-four in 1888 and spent most of his adult life in a somewhat tempestuous relationship with a married woman. It all ended in tears.

Not long before Easter 1884, Harry Jones got lodgings with the Harris family. He worked with Mr Harris at the Lucas & Aird's works and settled into the Harris home very quickly. It seems he was in bed with Mrs Harris within a couple of weeks. Not surprisingly, George Harris found out soon enough and was particularly annoyed about it all.

The trouble was that George Harris had a job that meant he had to spend long periods away from home. The thought of leaving his wife alone with Harry did not appeal. He knew that the moment his back was turned she would be straight into bed with him. He decided that the best idea was to send his wife to live in Gloucester, well away from Harry Jones. He regularly sent her money from wherever he was on his travels. Time passed and he lost track of Harry Jones.

One day he managed to get a chance to visit Sarah at Gloucester. He not only discovered that Harry was living with her, but she now had a daughter, Florence Mabel. There was, the newspapers said, some unpleasantness.

More time slid gracefully under the bridge, and Harry Jones, after some travelling, moved back to Aston, in February 1887. He was delighted to find that Sarah had moved into a house not far away and, even better, Mr Harris was working away again. Their liaison blossomed once more. By Christmas, Sarah was pregnant and Harry Jones had moved in. In March, Harry's

A typical court would have about six dwellings around a central yard. Such cramped conditions meant that everyone knew everyone else's business. Old and New Birmingham

second child was born, a bouncing baby boy, William Harold. They were now living in Sutherland Street, in a typical Birmingham court of small tenements surrounding a courtyard.

Although Harry may have been the bee's knees when it came to romancing Sarah Harris, he was pretty hopeless at providing adequate money, living off odd jobs here and there, sponging off Sarah in between times. Sarah was a woman who knew exactly which side her bread was buttered, and wasn't going to ditch her generous husband for a younger but penniless Harry.

The inevitable return of George Harris happened on Monday 11 June 1888. Harry's comfortable life ended abruptly as Sarah bundled him out of the house in such a hurry that he didn't even have time to grab his clothes. Harry managed to persuade old Mrs Wyatt across the courtyard to put him up for a few days. It was certainly not a good place to avoid meeting Mr Harris.

On the Tuesday, Harry was playing with little Florence in the kitchen of Mrs Wyatt's when Sarah came in. Harry told her that if she would throw his clothes down to him then he would go away and leave her in peace. No doubt she had a few choice words about his ability to earn his keep, because that afternoon he walked the nine miles to Oldbury to try and chase up an outstanding payment for a job. The people told him they would have the cash the following day, so he had to trudge back, sleep the night at Mrs Wyatt's and then walk all the way back on the Wednesday morning. He wasn't at all happy about the scornful way Sarah had chucked him out of the house and was in something of a black despairing mood because of his utter lack of prospects.

On his way back from Oldbury he passed down Steelhouse Lane, and went into William Banning's gun shop. There he purchased a revolver and six bullets. That evening he sat down and wrote a letter to his friend, Walter Wyatt. He sealed it up and gave it to another lodger in the house, one Charles Blackburn. The letter, which was opened just over a day later, gives an insight into Harry's mood that night:

The rabbits and pens belonging to Harry Benjamin Jones, I give them to Charles Blackburn or Walter Wyatt, and I also give the things that belong to me, H.B. Jones to Walter Wyatt and what he does not want I give to Charles Blackburn, as I see my life is a wreck and a ruin. God forgive me for what I have done in the world. I hope to meet my dear mother in heaven. When I am dead and gone the country will see I have been misled by a married woman who swore that she would never have anything to do with him (G.R. Harris) and she has sent for him just because I have happened to get a job, to walk nine miles night and morning, 18 miles to Oldbury. The two children belong to me, William Harold Harris, and I said to her, you go to register them yourself. I did not want to put the shame on her if I went to the register. That is all I have to say, good bye, God Bless you and may the Lord have mercy on my soul.

The invention of rim fire cartridges revolutionised handguns. This Irish model could be loaded and fired much faster that the old type. The guns became cheaper and more easily available. Arbour Antiques

The letter certainly seems to indicate that Harry Jones was contemplating suicide; he had bought the revolver, the bullets, left his worldly goods to his friends, and now all he needed to do was summon up the courage.

Thursday morning found Harry Jones pouring whisky down his throat like it was going out of fashion. He persuaded Charles Blackburn to go out and get another bottle several times. Gradually getting completely drunk, Harry brooded on his misfortunes, the peremptory way Sarah had treated him, the sheer unfairness of the way George Harris had come back. He lurched up from his chair and stormed into the yard. Charles followed him out.

Upstairs, Sarah heard the racket Harry was making and leant out of the window, throwing one of his collars down into the yard. Charles picked it up and Sarah shouted: 'Take it to the *****!' Harry threw it back at Sarah.

Mr Harris came out to see what on earth the noise was about. Harry took out the revolver and fired at him. Harris fled back into the house at some speed. Sarah was having none of this and stormed out. Harry fired a shot which caught her left shoulder. It appeared to have no effect on the enraged Sarah and she continued to advance on him. He fired again, this time catching her in the right shoulder. Sarah finally noticed she had been shot and dived behind Ellen Taman who had just wandered up to see what the racket was about. The two of them fell over and Harry came up and started beating Sarah on the head with the gun butt, saying: 'If I cannot shoot you, I'll knock your brains out.'

Ellen struggled to grab Harry to stop him and found herself staring down the barrel of the revolver. 'I'll serve you the same way,' he said. Ellen managed to wriggle out of the pile of fighting ex-lovers and run down the alleyway to shout for help. Harry shook himself free of Sarah, stood up and saw George Harris looking at him through the kitchen window. He fired two shots at him. They both missed, burying their burden of hatred into the brickwork.

He ran straight at the window and burst through it head first. George Harris was already out of the front door and ran down the street as fast as his legs could carry him. Inside was little Florence Mabel, standing just beside the table. The little mite was startled to see her father plunging into the room amid a shower of broken glass. She screamed and in a blind rage he smashed the gun barrel across her head. Florence was knocked under the table by the force of the blow. Harry paused momentarily and, looking at the broken and bleeding body of his daughter, decided to kill them all and be done with the whole damn thing. He ran up the stairs to the bedroom. There he found his son William Harold, just three months old, sleeping quietly in his cot. Savagely, he bashed the gun butt against his head.

Sarah, despite two gunshot wounds, rushed into the house to find her child, Florence, was unconscious, lying in a crumpled heap beneath the kitchen table. Upstairs, Harry was beating his baby son with the gun.

Exhausted, he stumbled back downstairs. Sarah darted back into the yard.

'I have killed the children and I'll kill you,' said Harry.

Sam Phillips had come running at the sound of the gunshots. He raced past Ellen and Sarah, grabbed Harry Jones and knocked the gun from his hand. Sarah was lucky, there was still one shot left. Alfred Hollis had also heard the ruckus and shots, picked up the gun, checked it and fired the last shot into the ground.

Mr Harris managed to find Police Inspector Hawkes in Lichfield Road and begged him to come and save them from this madman. When he entered the court Harry Jones came forward and said: 'I'm the man that has done it.' Inspector Hawkes arrested him.

A week later, Florence Mabel Harris died from the massive head injury Harry Jones had inflicted on her. The baby and his mother recovered from their wounds in time for the court case in August. Harry Jones, the drunken child-killer, died on the scaffold at Winson Green on 28 August 1888. There was no sympathy for him, no petitions for leniency.

CHAPTER 13

John Davis
1907

Jane Harrison burst through her front door, clutching her throat ...

The kind of murderous jealousy that appears so often in the pages of this book isn't only confined to young men and women. It can turn up in people who are supposedly older and wiser just as easily. The consequences are just as lethal. The story of how John Davis made his journey to the scaffold is a horribly familiar one. It all started in the bar of the *White Hart*, Cromwell Street, at the turn of the century.

John Davis was quite besotted with the landlady, Jane Harrison. This was rather more than the usual misty-eyed look that comes over most men looking at a barmaid. John was really fond of her and offered her plenty of emotional support as she went through a major trauma caused by her husband's mental breakdown and removal to Hatton Mental Asylum. With Edward gone, Jane found it increasingly difficult to manage the pub and had to move to Great Lister Street. John Davis visited her there often, to the intense annoyance of Jane's two grown up children who thought he was exploiting her. John's wife did know of his attachment, but seems not to have realised its depth for some time.

Edwin Harrison, Jane's eighteen-year-old son was still living at home, and one night he came back late to find Davis in the house. He made a scene and then went and got his sister and her husband to come back to the house with him. John Davis left promptly when they arrived. Edwin could not stand the man, and if he found a letter from him, he would throw it on the fire. The children soon passed details of the affair to John's wife. Mrs Davis called round to the house to give Jane Harrison a piece of her mind. It was all water off a ducks back to the couple and they continued to see each other intermittently. It seems likely that John was helping her financially.

John Davis had to move to Liverpool for a while. Jane Harrison was much reduced in her circumstances since her husband had been locked away and as she could no longer run the *White Hart* her income took a sharp turn for the worse. John was in Liverpool and so there was even less money. As Jane gradually descended into poverty she moved from the comparative comfort of Great Lister Street, first to John Street and finally to 17 Tower Place, one of the warren of squalid courts just off Tower Road, a stone's throw from Aston Cross.

Jane was earning what money she could as a cleaner and charwoman, and perhaps the occasional 'gentleman' helped her out. John Davis, although he came back from Liverpool from time to time, was unaware that she had other liaisons. This

Behind the gunshops of Steelhouse Lane lay a warren of run-down tenements which were mostly demolished in the 1880s. As Jane Harrison descended into poverty, slums like this were her only shelter. Old and New Birmingham

changed on the evening of Saturday 27 October 1906. That evening the forty-seven-year-old Jane Harrison met Mr Charles Hunter and the two of them went back to her house in Tower Place. After a while Jane went out to get a jug of beer. Charles Hunter waited for what seemed like ages, and resolved to go and see what had become of her. He followed her route towards the pub. He had not got far when found Jane and John Davis in heated argument in the street. Charles told Davis to beat it and he ran off in a jealous rage, convinced that Charles was Jane's 'Bully' or pimp.

Over the next couple of weeks Davis began lurking around Tower Place. None of the other families living in the crowded tenements knew Jane as anything other than a hard working mother; they had no idea of her long-standing relationship with Davis. It was with some surprise that they found him peering into their windows, loitering around the alley into the court and generally making a pest of himself.

This behaviour went on from 13 to 17 November. At about 10.30 on the Saturday morning Davis turned up at the front door and went in to talk to Jane. In the cramped confines of the court all the women who were at home could hear the sounds of raised voices in her house. Mrs McLackie, who lived next door couldn't quite make out what the two of them were arguing about, but it didn't sound terribly serious. It might have sounded like eavesdropping but in the midst of these poverty-ridden hovels the women looked after each other as best they could. No one else was going to.

Twenty minutes passed, and a sudden, terrible shriek echoed through the brick-lined yard. Jane Harrison burst through her front door, clutching her throat, blood pouring through her hands.

'What shall I do?' she whimpered.

Mrs McLackie and the other women poured from their houses. They grabbed hold of Jane and guided her into Mrs McLackie's.

John Davis sauntered out of the door a few moments afterwards.

'Stop him!' The uproar could be heard over most of Aston. The beerhouse-keeper over the road had a police whistle and blew it for all his worth. John Davis was surrounded by a mob of

MYSTERIOUS CRIME AT ASTON.

WOMAN MURDERED IN HER HOME.

A STRANGE VISITOR.

NEIGHBOURS ARREST THE ACCUSED MAN.

furious women and could not escape. Mrs McLackie ran for Doctor Hunter and PC Parker sprinted along the street to restore order. He found Davis held firmly in the grip of Mr Edwards. Davis was promptly handcuffed. One of the women shrieked that he had cut Jane's throat with a razor. Davis shrugged and pointed at his pocket; in it PC Parker found the bloodstained razor. Doctor Hunter and Inspector Hawkes arrived quickly. There was little the doctor could do to stem the bleeding from a massive gash across the woman's neck. He called for the Fire Brigade's ambulance to take her to the General Hospital, but Jane died within a few minutes of getting there.

John Davis was brought to trial before Justice Ridley on 10 December 1906. His rather pathetic defence was that he was actually having a shave in the house when Jane complained of a dreadful headache, grabbed his hand holding the razor, and drew it across her own throat. His defence lawyer had brought a series of letters from Jane to John that were purported to show that she had suicidal tendencies. Justice Ridley read them all through and told the defence team that for every one that might be interpreted in this way, there were twenty that could not. He refused to allow them as evidence. When the jury returned the guilty verdict he had no hesitation in sending John Davis to the gallows. He was hanged at Winson Green on 1 January 1907, aged fifty-three.

CHAPTER 14

William Allen Butler
1916

He pointed to the slumped body of Florence.

Once again the green-eyed demon of jealousy led to the untimely demise of another Birmingham woman. Florence Beatrice Butler got married when she was about twenty, in 1905. The marriage wasn't a success and, by 1910, she was back living with her mother, Mrs Griffiths, at 2 Bath Terrace, off Chequers Walk. She had a daughter by this marriage, one Nellie Butler, who was born in 1907.

As ever in the harsh economic climate of the era, Florence had to make ends meet as best she could. Her mother took in lodgers to help the family finances as well. It was one of the lodgers that caused all the trouble. William Allen Butler moved in as a lodger in July 1915. Although he had the same surname, he was not related to the family in any way. He was a thirty-nine-year-old brass-caster.

It wasn't long before William and Florence were on very friendly terms indeed. William rapidly got the impression that he was the only man in Florence's life and that she was his *de facto* wife. It was a relationship that he felt was confirmed by the announcement of Florence's pregnancy in the early months of 1916. There isn't much evidence that Florence saw things in this light at all. She still had at least one regular visitor who treated her every now and then. If William knew about old Mr Ireland he kept his mouth shut, quite possibly because being cuckolded by a sixty-nine year old wouldn't do his credibility much good.

Jealousy is a vicious, nasty vice and it isn't always confined to rival lovers either. There is a particularly loathsome sort of man who seems to get jealous of an unborn child. Every expecting

Even in the middle of the First World War the city was a bustling hive of activity.
Author's collection

mum gives more and more attention to that little growing lump
and some men can't cope with the competition.

Florence went and had a long talk with her mother in the
second week of May 1916. William had started beating her. A
few days later she showed her mother the bruises that covered
her legs. Like a typical bully and coward he had hit her where it
wouldn't show. Florence's mother went berserk. William, who
was in the room at the time, was told to find himself somewhere
else to live as soon as he possibly could. The quarrel was heard
by most of the street.

The quarrel continued on the 20th, but seemed to cool off
by lunchtime, perhaps because there were no more plates left
to throw. Mrs Griffiths was adamant that William was to leave.
No one was going to treat her daughter like that. William had
arranged to meet Florence in town that evening. He had an
afternoon nap and went to meet her at about 9 o'clock. There
was no sign of her and he returned to the house at about
10.00 pm. Florence had returned a short while before. William
demanded to know where she had been.

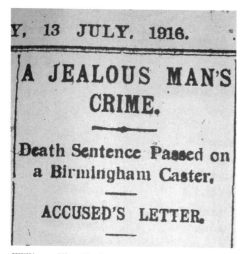

Y, 13 JULY, 1916.

A JEALOUS MAN'S CRIME.

Death Sentence Passed on a Birmingham Caster.

ACCUSED'S LETTER.

William Allen Butler. Birmingham Gazette

'I have been with Mr Ireland. He bought me this crab which is more than you ever would do, and if you don't shut your mouth I will smack your face.'

Old Mrs Griffiths was upstairs making the beds, their neighbour Mrs Rice had gone home; there was just William, Florence and little Nellie downstairs.

Boiling with rage and jealousy, William pulled a clasp knife from his coat pocket, took a couple of strides across to room to where Florence was sitting and plunged it straight through her left breast into her heart.

Mrs Griffiths came running downstairs at the sound of Nellie's screams. William was just storming out of the house. 'What have you done?' she shouted.

'What I have done is what I said I would do before.' He pointed at the slumped body of Florence.

Somehow, the old lady managed to get her to Maria Keating's house next door, but it was too late to help Florence; she was dead within fifteen minutes.

William Butler stood outside for a few moments and decided to ask one of his friends down the street what on earth he should do now. He showed them the blood-splattered knife. They very sensibly offered to call the police.

'It is not necessary; I will go to the police station and give myself up.' He wandered off into the night. He seems to have then bumped into a policeman in Broad Street who directed him to Ladywood Station and, at five past eleven, he turned up there and handed himself over to PC Sheraston.

'I want to give myself up for stabbing my wife with a knife,' he said.

PC Sheraston was somewhat taken aback and asked: 'When did you do this?'

'Just now; I came straight up here. I told the policeman in Broad Street I meant to do it,' he was told.

If PC Sheraston held any doubts about whether this was a stunt or prank, they were soon dispelled by the letter that William had in his pocket. It was addressed to his mother:

20 May – Dear Mother, we like one another, but it is better to part sooner or later, as I am sick of my life.

Justice was a lot quicker in those difficult days during the First World War. William Butler was in court on 12 July and sentenced to death after a short hearing. On 16 August in Winson Green Prison, John Ellis, the state executioner, performed the fatal sentence. For the man who beat and eventually killed his girlfriend there were no petitions or mourners apart from his own heartbroken mother.

CHAPTER 15

Henry Gaskin, the Hednesford Ripper
1919

There was now another, primordial darkness in those pupils.

The long-term effects of the First World War were not confined to peace treaties and international politics. Thousands upon thousands of ordinary people found their lives destroyed in countless ways. There were widows everywhere, factories and mines were desperate for staff and our economy was crippled by the vast expense. Another and far more insidious side effect was the mental anguish of some, and the utter brutalisation of others. The carnage of the trenches left deep scars.

Henry Thomas Gaskin was a bright enough lad before the war. He was born in 1892 to a reasonably well off working class family. He grew up slightly hyperactive but a keen sportsman and leader of the newly-formed Boy Scouts. Gaskin gained notoriety when he covered himself in feathers and rode through the village dressed as a Red Indian. It was probably his natural high spirits that attracted the girls to him. Henry Gaskin married his sweetheart, Elizabeth Talbot, in July 1913. She was four years his junior. Their first child was born that December.

The marriage may have been cursed from the beginning. For some unknown reason, the newspapers never disclosed it, Henry was taken away by the authorities in May 1914. In May 1916, he joined the army and was posted to the trenches in France, without even being given the chance to return home to see his wife and child. Henry did well in the army, his high spirits meant he was popular and he was promoted to Sergeant. All very well until the day a mine went off underneath him. He came back to Hednesford in September 1917, to recuperate.

Elizabeth had not exactly lived the life of a nun whilst he was gone. She had gained a certain reputation, and a couple more children to prove it. Living on her own with the kids was difficult so she had moved back to her mother's house at Brindley Heath. Henry seemed to be oblivious to the various children of whom he could not be the father, and appears to have stayed with the family until his return to the war. Weary and shell shocked, he couldn't summon the strength to sort matters out with Elizabeth. Back at the Front he appeared to have become totally fearless and utterly reckless of his own safety, even in the most intense shell fire. Perhaps he sought a glorious death as release from the complexity and humiliation of his family affairs. Death eluded him amongst the whirring shards of shrapnel and crisp cordite concussions. Death had other plans for Henry Thomas Gaskin.

Henry returned home from the trenches a much more sober man. He was a tall, sturdily-built character with a shock of curly black hair, but the mischievous twinkle of his teenage days had gone. Like so many others of his generation, those eyes had seen into an abyss of unspeakable horror. There was now another, primordial darkness in those pupils.

In January 1919, Elizabeth gave birth to yet another child, apparently fathered by 'Monty' Harris. It wasn't quite the home-coming Henry had anticipated on his de-mob. He moved in with his mother at Bridgetown, some three miles away, on 1 February and started work at a nearby colliery, West Cannock Pit. He made it clear to Elizabeth that he wanted a divorce on the grounds of infidelity. She really didn't want this to happen and repeatedly tried to persuade him to change his mind. He was adamant and for all his apparently laissez faire attitude of September 1917, he was utterly furious at her behaviour and the litter of bastard children she had produced during his absence.

On Wednesday 19 February, Gaskin and some mates were drinking in the *Angelesey Arms*. Henry was not a noted drinker but that morning he seemed to be knocking it back with a vengeance, steeling his nerve for something. Henry gave a note to his friend, Thomas Saunders, with the instructions to take it to Elizabeth. It was brief: 'Meet me round the pool at once –

important.' Saunders delivered it to Elizabeth and she went to meet Henry at 2 o'clock.

The pool was beside the Hednesford to Rugeley road, next to the Cannock & Rugeley Colliery Company offices; further up Hednesford Hill was a spinney of densely planted trees. It was a bleak and deserted part of the country. Nevertheless, Elizabeth and Henry were seen arguing by the side of the road. The witness, Mr Borton, saw Henry walk off towards the wood and Elizabeth walk off in the opposite direction. A brief while later she was seen walking alongside the wood and not far behind her, running after her, in a low crouch, was Henry Gaskin. It was the last time she was seen alive.

Emily Talbot became seriously worried when Elizabeth failed to return. Emily told the police that her daughter was missing that evening. She also asked Henry Gaskin what he had done with her; that she knew of their meeting by the pool and would inform the police. The search for the slender, 5 feet tall, twenty-three-year-old girl started the next morning. The pool was dragged and the woods searched but with no sign of her whatsoever.

Throughout Thursday, the search went on with no sign of Elizabeth. Friday morning, however, brought a surprise. Emily Talbot received a letter. It was from a Mr Brookes and stated that Lizzie was with him in Birmingham, she was perfectly all right and not to worry. If anything it made her even more worried. She knew her daughter was prone to going off with other men, but not to just vanish, leaving her seven-week-old baby alone. She called the police straight away. They examined the letter, checked the handwriting and decided that they needed to talk to Henry Thomas Gaskin. They found him working at the colliery that evening and questioned him. Gaskin's answers were confused and he denied meeting Elizabeth on the Wednesday afternoon. They knew this was a lie and arrested him on suspicion of murder.

The police searched Gaskin as a matter of course when he was brought into the police station. They were alarmed to find a large clasp knife in his pocket. It was heavily bloodstained. Superintendent Murray and Inspector Woolley started to question Gaskin but could get nothing out of him other than a complete denial that he had seen Elizabeth on the Wednesday. Out in the countryside the search covered a wider area but found no trace of the girl.

The bloodstained knife gave Inspector Woolley every reason to keep Gaskin in custody when he was brought before a special court in Cannock on the Saturday. Once again all Gaskin said was: 'All I can say is I did not see her.' The magistrate wasn't in the least bit convinced and granted Inspector Woolley's request to keep Gaskin on remand.

Gaskin must have realised that he was without any shred of a defence and on the Sunday afternoon asked for an interview with the Inspector. The policeman might have thought he had encountered pretty much everything in his years of police work, but as Gaskin confessed in minute detail exactly what he had done with Elizabeth, the blood drained from his face. Here was a catalogue of utter horror such as even he had never even conceived.

Gaskin had attacked Elizabeth at the edge of the spinney and dragged her into the dense trees. There, hidden by the thick bushes, he had kicked and punched her repeatedly. When her screams became too loud, he shoved a branch down her throat.

The rough scrubland at the edge of Cannock Chase was the scene of the most unspeakable violence. Author's collection

He then took out his clasp knife and stabbed and slashed at her belly until one of her legs was virtually cut off, her head was completely severed from her body and still he hacked at her now lifeless corpse, effectively eviscerating her.

By dusk, his maniacal blood-lust was sated and he started to wonder how he could dispose of the body. He went home and got a wheelbarrow, but by now a flurry of snow had left a light layer on the ground. He returned to the spinney, gathered up her clothes and made the first of several journeys back towards Hednesford. The first journey started off with all the bits in the barrow, but he realised that the wheel was leaving a deep track in the snow and he gave up on that idea. He carried the wreckage of the poor girl by hand. He dumped the clothes, her head and other bits of her body into the well of an abandoned gasometer close to Hednesford pool, just behind the railway station. The water in the well was 18 feet deep, but to be sure that Elizabeth's body couldn't float up to the surface in a few days, he skewered what was left of her body with a heavy length of lead gas pipe before consigning it to the dark oily water.

Henry Gaskin should have remembered the old adage about revenge: before you start you should dig two graves – one for your victim, and one for yourself.

On Monday morning, the police hired a taxi and took Henry out to the spinney. There he pushed aside the brambles and bushes to show them the bloodstained scene of the butchery. They then travelled back to Hednesford and he led them to the gasometer well. It was only a few minutes before they managed to rake out some of Elizabeth's clothes. His story confirmed, Henry was returned to the station whilst the police obtained longer rakes to thoroughly dredge the well. Within an hour they retrieved the horrifically mutilated body, but it was a day or so before they managed to recover her head.

Henry's only defence when the case came to court in August was that he was insane. He sat through the hearing completely unmoved; barely a muscle flickered on his face even when the judge pronounced the death sentence. The defence of insanity completely failed to convince the jury, who took only twenty minutes to agree he was guilty of wilful murder. It was obvious that Gaskin had extracted a fiendishly fearful revenge on his wife because of her infidelity. This was no sudden outburst of emotion; he had plotted to lure her to an isolated spot, and further plotted to allay every suspicion against him by sending the letter saying she had gone to Birmingham.

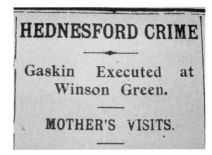

HEDNESFORD CRIME

Gaskin   Executed   at
Winson   Green.

MOTHER'S VISITS.

Henry Gaskin. Birmingham Gazette

Justice Roche summed up the case, saying: 'Heaven forbid that one should seek to encourage or excuse marital infidelity, but if grown people of ripe age elected to sin in that way, the State had not made that sin a crime punishable by law and still less had it thought fit to make it a crime punishable by death.'

What was punishable by death was the callous killing of one's wife. On 8 August, at Winson Green Prison, Henry Gaskin was hanged by the executioner, John Ellis. A crowd of 200 waited outside the gates shortly before 8 o'clock in the morning. A minute or two after 8.00, the prison bell tolled. Several minutes later a guard emerged from the gate and stuck two notices up. The first stated: 'Judgment of death was this day executed on Henry Thomas Gaskin.' It was signed by F A Bolton, Sheriff of Staffordshire. The second was to the effect that the prison surgeon, Dr W Cassels, had examined the body and found that it was definitely dead. John Ellis knew his trade, Gaskin died instantly.

So it would seem that the sorry tale ends, but not quite. The dense spinney is still there, the last mute witness to one of the most horrific murders the district has ever known.

CHAPTER 16

The Remarkable Story of Djang Djin Sung
1919

The man had been beaten about the head with a hammer ...

One of Birmingham's most prolific authors was the son of an Irish immigrant family. Arthur Henry Ward was born in 1883 to a working class family, received virtually no formal education until he was nine and published his first work in 1913. The book captured the mood of the age and created an infamous villain whose name echoes down the annals of crime fiction to this day. Better known by his pen-name, Sax Rohmer, he invented the diabolically evil Dr Fu Manchu.

This was an era when the British empire was still unsure of the Chinese empire, the dreaded Yellow Peril. Our society was deeply suspicious of foreigners and Sax Rohmer's tales of the oriental mastermind, with his cruel cunning, secret societies and mysterious occult powers pandered to the popular preconceptions of the age. Like most of the popular literature of the day, the stories are blatantly racist and the stiff upper lipped hero, Denis Nayland Smith, always wins. That said, they are cracking good adventures and make marvellous films!

Birmingham in 1919 did not have dismal docks infested with swarthy oriental gangsters plotting to take over the world, as Sax Rohmer would have us believe London did. Nevertheless, Birmingham had its canal docks, teeming factories and a massive labour shortage which was rapidly filled after the war by a new influx of immigrants – the Chinese. Like the Irish before them, they found the cheapest accommodation, and in much the same way, a few rotten eggs slipped in with the thousands of

Sax Rohmer's character, Dr Fu Manchu, coloured an entire generation's view of the Chinese. Author's collection

honest labourers. The Chinese tended to keep to themselves and this aloofness tended to reinforce the xenophobic attitudes portrayed in Rohmer's books. Everyone was ready to believe in his fantasy world of squalid opium dens, triad killings, black-mail and white slavery.

Djang Djin Sung was twenty-three, worked at Briscoe & Co and spent a while lodging with Mrs Alice Grosvenor at 248 Pershore Road. He was just one of the many Chinese who lodged there. Another boarding house overcrowded with Chinese lodgers was 109 Coleshill Street. It was from here that Zee Ming Wu went missing on 24 June. Li Ding Jig was the person who reported that he hadn't turned up for work that day.

The next day, Djang Djin Sung also mentioned the missing man to his landlord, in fact the whole crowd of Chinese lodgers were now terrified and begged Mr Grosvenor to sleep in the room with them for protection. Something very nasty had happened to frighten that many people. Just how nasty was discovered on 27 June.

A young boy called Henry Wilson was playing in Warley Park when he found the hideously mutilated body of Zee Ming Wu partially hidden behind a tree. The man had been beaten about the head with a hammer, thoroughly enough to kill him. He had also been cut about the genitals in some kind of ritual revenge. It was no surprise that there was a palpable air of terror in the Chinese community. The police enquires were painfully slow to start with. An almost insuperable barrier was the very poor English most of the Chinese spoke, particularly if they weren't feeling cooperative.

Zee Ming Wu was a surprisingly wealthy man. He had £240 in his post office savings account. This account was held at the West Kensington post office and it was there, on 24 June, that a suspicious looking Chinaman had tried to withdraw the entire amount. The cashier looked at the book and queried the identity of the man asking for all the money. He then told him that they would have to go to the police station to verify that all was in order. The man panicked and tried to grab the book back, but the cashier held on to it tightly. The man then said he would return with proper identification and walked away hurriedly.

The crime in Warley Woods was not immediately linked to the attempted theft of Zu Ming Wu's money for some time. The Birmingham police were finding a wall of terrified silence obstructed their investigation. The London police had the details of the murder and the attempt to withdraw the money, but had no leads to follow. As is often the way, yet another crime opened a can of worms that resolved the mystery.

Djang Djin Sung was arrested following an altercation with Kuo Doung Dsou in Aldine Street, Shepherd's Bush. For some reason or other, Djang Djin Sung was trying to kill the other man. He had been under immense pressure for the last month and finally snapped into a homicidal rage at Kuo. The police arrested him for affray, and discovered Zu Ming Wu's bank book in his pocket.

Djang Djin Sung was charged with the murder of Zu Ming Wu and decided to confess his knowledge of the whole affair, thinking that this would prove that he was not guilty of the murder, even if he was complicit in the deed and had been the man attempting to empty the Post Office account. He didn't know at the time that the police had also found the hammer used in the murder at the place where he had been staying in

London. The confession was reported verbatim in the news-papers of the day. I suspect that it wouldn't hold up in court today, but it is a fascinating glimpse into the course of justice in 1919:

I wantee tellee very true I have a very good mother and four good brothers. I wantee tellee true because such a disgrace in my country to tell lies to big chief (Detective Inspector Savage, Paddington) I went to work at Briscoe's on 23rd June and left at half past five. Four Chinamen, Ling Ding Son (or Jig), Zoo Zing Bar, Ling Gai Wu and Zing Ming Wu met me. Ling Gai Wu asked me to pinch hammer. They said don't tell anyone, go and pinch hammer.

I went back into work and pinched hammer. Ling Ding Son asked me first to pinch hammer. When I pinched the hammer I gave the hammer to Ling Ding Son, and he and I together took a tram car, went a long way to a lonely park, and the killed man came together with us. Zoo Zing Bar and Ling Gai Wu came on the next car. The three of us walked together till we got to the big trees. It was about 7 o'clock or quarter past seven at this time.

Ling Ding Son told me that the killed man's father and brother, good business and good learning, had cheated him out of money in police court in China and he said he was going to killee Zee Ming Wu. The other two Chinamen were following on behind, nearly there, not far behind. Ling Ding Son said to killed man 'Lookee, lookee, lookee, big mappi, mappi (rabbit).'

The killed man look, I look as well, and Ling Ding Son hit him on the head with a hammer, and he say nothing at all. He fell down and he gave him one, two three terrible with hammer. The other two came up – Zoo Zing Bar and Ling Gai Wu. I took the bank book from the lining of the coat of the killed man at the back. Ling Ding Son told me he carried his money there.

I, with Ling Ding Son and Ling Gai Wu carried the killed man not far away under big tree, Zoo Zing Bar looked on and said 'Very Dirty, plenty, plenty, quick, quick go away' Zoo Zing Bar said 'All go home by self, must not be together.' Zoo Zing Bar and Ling Gai Wu went away together because they would speak best English, and I picked up hammer and came away with Ling Ding Son.

We all met together at New Street and spoke for about half an hour, and they then told me to go to London with the bank book next day to get the money. Ling Ding Son said he was going to work next day. Other two never work.

I went to London on Tuesday 24th. Went to Post Office at West Kensington about 2 o'clock or 3 o'clock; waited there half an hour. I looked at killed man's name and address in the book and wrote it on paper at Post Office. I cannot get money as man said I go Police Station. I frightened; tried to pull back book: couldn't get it backee. I tell him I get back soon and walk away quick.

I go back to Birmingham very soon, about 4 o'clock and went home. When I got back to Birmingham station Zoo Zing Bar and Ling Gai Wu were waiting for me. On Friday 27th I see in newspapers about killee man and cannot sleep; and I asked Mr Grosvenor to sleep with me. All the other men were frightened like me. Ling Ding Son stopped in Birmingham to work. Zoo Zing Bar came to London Tuesday or Wednesday.

The police had no hesitation in charging Ding Djang Sung with the murder. Ling Ding Jig (or Son) had an alibi for the night in question. He stood in the witness box calm and confident that he could not be prosecuted. He stated that he had overheard a conversation between Djang Djin Sung and Zee Ming Wu where Djang offered to pay Zee thirty shillings, a debt that was

The forbidding gatehouse of Winson Green Prison. It was the last glimpse of the world for many of the characters in this book. John Marks collection

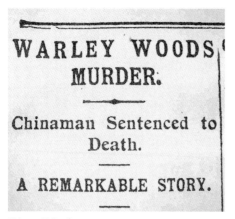

Djang Djin Sung. Birmingham Gazette

outstanding. Zee replied that he had enough money at the moment. His alibi was confirmed by Theresa Mascol who swore that he had been in his lodgings at 109 Coleshill Street all of the Monday night.

As Ling Ding Jig stepped down from the witness box, Djang Djin Sung could contain himself no longer and burst out: 'My Lord, the murderer, not me!'

It did him no good. Mr Justice Rowlatt was having none of it. He had been involved in the killing from the very outset and that was quite enough to send him to the gallows. The jury agreed.

The court case ended on 22 October and on 3 December Djang Djin Sung paid the ultimate price for his involvement with the gang. John Ellis hanged him in Winson Green Prison.

CHAPTER 17

Samuel Westwood 1920

I have stabbed my wife ...

The emotional repercussions of the First World War were felt for decades after the Armistice. The idea of the horrors of the war lingering in the minds and behaviour of the participants seems to have been disregarded by the medical profession of the day, so there was no treatment other than a quick 'Pull yourself together man.'

Samuel Westwood was probably considered a lucky man only to have been knocked unconscious by an exploding shell, even if he was captured afterwards. This was towards the end of the war, in 1918, so he had had plenty of time to see the full devastation that the conflict had wreaked on an entire generation. His injuries from the explosion weren't too bad and it wasn't long before the Germans forced him to work down a mine, treating him like a virtual slave for eight months.

Samuel was a very short tempered man when he returned to his parents' house in Bentley Lane, Short Heath, after the war. Nevertheless, he managed to get himself a job as a key filer and started to build his life all over again. Times were pretty hard in 1920 and when he started walking out with Lydia Vaughan their future seemed bleak. It would be difficult to set up a house together on his meagre earnings. He was twenty-six and she was twenty-four.

This didn't stop them getting married at the end of July. The trouble was that they had to move into Samuel's parents' house, filling the small cottage to overflowing. It really didn't work well ... it seldom does. Lydia argued with Samuel's mother on a nearly daily basis, pushing Samuel into increasingly violent outbursts of temper. By the time a month and a half had passed Lydia had packed her bags and gone back to her mother's house in Cross Street, Spring Bank, Willenhall. This was on Thursday 9 September.

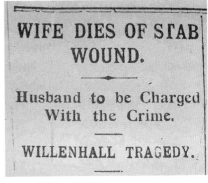

WIFE DIES OF STAB WOUND.

Husband to be Charged With the Crime.

WILLENHALL TRAGEDY.

Samuel Westwood. Birmingham Gazette

A couple of days passed and Lydia had probably forgotten the worst of the rows and overcrowding; she just wanted to see her beloved Samuel again. Alice Vaughan, her mother, was deeply suspicious and didn't really want to see her daughter getting involved with the fiery tempered young man. Lydia persuaded her that they should go to the fair to find him on Saturday 11 September. On the day the two of them wandered about Wakes Ground in Walsall Street amid the stalls until they found him.

Earnestly talking about the future, the three of them left the fair and walked into Church Street. There they stood for a long time, Lydia and Samuel trying to patch up their problems and Lydia's mother wondering whether this was a recipe for disaster. She kept butting in and generally trying to manipulate her daughter into refusing to go back to her husband. Samuel Westwood, temper already frayed to breaking point, looked from one woman to the other, unsure of what to believe, what the future would be. An increasingly frustrated and bewildered mood closed in around Samuel. He pulled a heavy clasp knife from his pocket and lashed out in a boiling rage.

It isn't clear whether he meant to stab Lydia or her interfering mother. The result was a single massive wound in Lydia's neck, completely severing her jugular vein. As the blood gushed from the mortal wound Samuel walked briskly to the police station in Walsall Street.

'I have stabbed my wife down the road,' he calmly informed Sergeant Evans in the station yard. The officer took one look at his blood-covered hand, then sprinted out of the station and down the road to where Lydia was lying. There was nothing he could do for her; she was breathing her last.

The trial attracted little publicity. The public were getting unpleasantly familiar with stories of returning soldiers venting their pent up anguish on their wives, families or themselves.

His defence tried to explain that he had been driven partially insane by his experiences but it was to an unsympathetic jury. He was found guilty on 19 November and executed on the 30 December at Winson Green, yet another 'victim' of the Great War.

CHAPTER 18

Elijah Pountney
1922

Blood erupted from the severed arteries.

The demon drink seems to crop up quite regularly in most books about murder. Although, quite often, it is only a convenient excuse for someone who just couldn't be bothered to go through the ordinary divorce process. There have always been alcoholics, and quite a few of them have been seriously unhinged. Elijah Pountney was a thoroughly inebriated alcoholic. The trouble for an alcoholic running a pub is that it is very much kill or cure. In this case it was his wife that got killed and he was cured on the scaffold.

Elijah Pountney and his wife, Alice Gertrude, ran the *Pheasant Inn*, a very small and old pub in Broad Street, Bilston, since 1916. Elijah was forty-eight years old in 1922 and worked

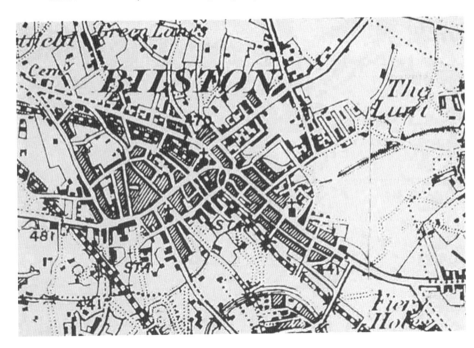

as a blacksmith at the Tarmac Works. It was Alice that ran the pub. He had spent at least the last six months drunk. It didn't take a lot to get him drunk these days; about a year before he had been hit on the head by a falling cinder block and been rather strange ever since. A couple of pints and he was fighting drunk, although not usually capable of doing much about it. In this year, he had become far more quarrelsome and started beating his wife.

This did not impress Alice's brother, although one may wonder just how much he cared for her by the remark: 'You may use her as a punch-ball but not as a football.' Her son, John Edward, was often round the pub to try and stop the arguments. He lived not far away in Sankey Street.

Anyway, it wasn't a scene of domestic harmony that pervaded the *Pheasant Inn* when Mr Edmund McCann took up lodgings there in the autumn of 1921. It wasn't long before Elijah was first suspicious and then convinced that something was going on between Alice and the new lodger. He fancied that he had overheard them talking about running away together. McCann probably felt sorry for Alice, he had frequently seen her abused and hit by Elijah, but he certainly had no romantic affection towards the forty-seven-year-old landlady. Alice on the other hand, made sure that her lodger was fed properly, sometimes getting a better supper than her drunken sot of a husband. Elijah fumed about the imagined infidelity and eventually tried to get the police to evict McCann on 3 March. The police had no authority to do so and had to put up with a tirade of invective from Elijah. He made the mistake of saying that if McCann stayed he would end up killing Alice. The police didn't take the threat seriously, but bore it mind anyway.

Matters weren't improved by Elijah's drinking. By Easter 1922 he had been on a six month 'bender' and unable to distinguish fact from fantasy. He had become convinced that Alice was now pregnant with McCann's child, and that she had lent him money. The beatings he gave her were real enough though, and everyone knew it.

Easter Sunday lunchtime at the *Pheasant Inn* was a pretty quiet affair, by now virtually all the locals had gone elsewhere not wishing to be involved in the constant squabbling. The only customer in the bar was Joseph Henry Norton and he was a long-standing family friend. Elijah was as thoroughly drunk as usual. He and Alice were in the kitchen peeling potatoes with her son, John. Elijah and Alice had been quarrelling all morning, as usual.

Joseph Norton decided it was time to leave and called out from the bar: 'Elijah, what time are you shutting?' Elijah said nothing but Alice called out: 'Come here Joe.' Elijah muttered something as Joseph entered the kitchen and Alice pointed the potato peeler at him and said to him: 'If it wasn't for this lad [she indicated her son] I would . . .' and she gestured with the knife. Elijah looked at Joseph and said to him: 'Kiss her, Joe. It will be the last time.' Elijah walked across the kitchen and up to Alice: 'Come here,' he said, and went to embrace her, his right arm curling around her shoulders.

John thought he was going to kiss his mother, but in a flash realised that Elijah was holding an open razor in his hand. He leapt to her side but even as he rose Elijah ripped the wickedly sharp blade right through her throat. Blood erupted from the severed arteries. She collapsed backwards a few paces into John's arms. He dragged her out through the door onto the veranda, but in that short space of time she had bled to death.

Joseph Norton sprinted down the road to fetch a doctor and Elijah walked out of the house. The way that he casually wiped his hands on a bit of newspaper and threw the razor into the fireplace before he left gave a clue to his callous state of mind. He disappeared off in the direction of his mother's house in Bradley.

As Joseph Norton sprinted towards Dr Mathie's surgery he called to the policeman on point duty in the road. The constable sent another policeman to raise the alarm at the station whilst he ran to the *Pheasant*. The doctor arrived shortly after, but there was nothing he could do for Alice, she was dead. Superintendent Higgs and several other officers arrived at the scene. The last anyone had seen of Elijah was him running down the road to Bradley, so Sergeants Cartwright and Daniels set off in pursuit.

Down by the canal a gang of boys had spotted a bottle floating in the water and were getting some stones to try and sink it. One of them noticed a strange thing, there was a man wedged between a couple of coal boats, just his head showing

SON SEES MOTHER KILLED.

Domestic Tragedy At Bilston.

HUSBAND CHARGED WITH MURDER.

Bilston, a small Staffordshire township near Wolverhampton, was the scene yesterday of a terrible domestic tragedy. Alice Gertrude Pountney, wife of Elijah Pountney, a well-known local publican, is dead, and the latter is under arrest and will be charged

... led his ...

Afterwards the man threw a mile, and speedily threw off him to drown himself in the canal near Bradley, but he was rescued by some boys, and collapsed into a state of semi-consciousness just before the arrival of police officers who were in pursuit. Doctors were called, and the man recovered sufficiently, after artificial respiration had been applied, to be

...POUTS!

Scanned ... Saw Nine me.

A remarkable spout is related ... s Carston ... his return ... Cuba. Near the naval ... vessel ran into ... and the sea became ... waterspouts were ... away, and another ... hundred yards ... closing down on it. The helm was put ... and the ship just kept ... ing water from the ... contact with it, the wat... lower half crashing ... There were at this time ... nine large spouts within ... the ship. When the nearest side of ... abeam it was not more than ... distant, and the row it ... indescribable. There were ol... men on board, but none had ... before.

FOR A DOG.

Brove ... Major Pou...

Major Cecil Walker, late of the ... a London estate ... who was spending Easter with relatives in Peterborough, was drowned in the River Nene on Satur...

LATE BISH COVENT

Funeral To Ta In Wiltsh

CREATED TV

The funeral of the la Biggs, Bishop of Coventr at 2 p.m. on Wednesday shire, where Mrs. Ye buried in 1909.

It is probable that a se simultaneously in Coven His death took place Swanage after an ill months. Deceased was

A cross, surmounted A Bishop's throne at t l. Many had expect crepe, but the Su chappell), decided t were a happier s...

he Cathedral yest ed the late Bis a sympathetic a great organi...

Elijah Pountney. Birmingham Gazette

out of the black water. They ran down to the canal bank and with the help of another couple of lads, managed to drag Pountney onto the road. He spluttered water and they asked him where he lived and he replied he didn't know, but knew his way home. He staggered off along the road and then veered back towards the canal. The boys followed to see what would happen next. Pountney collapsed in a heap before he got to the water.

The two policemen arrived, one of them quickly started to give Pountney the kiss of life whilst the other raced off to get Doctor Waddell. The doctor arrived quickly and, with his assistance, they managed to revive the suicidal man. Luckily a motor car came passed and they flagged it down. They managed to get Pountney into the security and warmth of the police station before he got hypothermia. He was charged with murdering his wife and hustled off to the infirmary at the workhouse.

The trial started on 7 July. Pountney's defence was that he was in no condition to have been able to premeditate a murder because he was drunk. He should be charged with manslaughter because it was an unpremeditated act triggered in part by his head injury and the alcohol. The prosecution quite rightly pointed out that he had threatened to kill her on numerous occasions before the dreadful deed was committed, and that there were plenty of witnesses who had seen him kicking and beating his wife in the *Pheasant*. Dr Hamblin Smith, the medical officer at Winson Green Gaol, said that he had interviewed Pountney and found him quite rational.

The jury found him guilty of wilful murder and Mr Justice Shearman pronounced the death sentence. Elijah Pountney's only comment was: 'I don't remember any of it.'

Elijah Pountney was hanged in Winson Green Gaol on 11 August by the state executioner, John Ellis. A sorry end for a sorry character.

CHAPTER 19

The Small Heath Tragedy 1926

... he went upstairs and banged the old lady on the head with a knuckled stick ...

Ada Taylor was having trouble with John Fisher. It had taken many years to really brew up but in October 1926 she had finally had enough. He was just bone idle. Ada let him move in with her after her good-for-nothing husband walked out back in 1910, leaving her with an eight-year-old daughter and precious little to survive on.

Over the years John Fisher seemed to do less and less. He scrounged money off her and even off her daughter Jessie when she was old enough to earn her own cash. His last known job was in 1923 and he had been on the dole ever since. He was a trained machinist, but didn't let that stop him leading a life of indolence. He had managed to get himself discharged from the Marines because of epilepsy when he much younger. Now he was fifty-eight and their future was looking very bleak indeed.

By October, Ada had sought an ejectment order to get him out of the house and it was only a matter of days before he was due to leave. On Sunday 25 October John decided he needed a spot of cash and, not having anything in his pockets, decided to pawn the family tablecloth. Not surprisingly there was an almighty row over Sunday lunch.

Sunday afternoon at No. 1 Back, 27 Wright Street was a particularly silent one. Jessie had come round for lunch with her mum. She had long since grown up and got married to Mr Dutton. John's usual Sunday chore was to sharpen the cutlery and kitchen knives and while he was doing it a wicked thought crept into his mind: 'Why not kill them all?' He thought about how it would solve his problems.

Jessie Dutton, blithely unaware that across the room John Fisher was planning to kill her, decided to go out at 4 o'clock. Ada Taylor said she felt like an afternoon nap and went upstairs as Jessie closed the door behind her. John Fisher was temporarily flummoxed, his first victim had just gone off for an afternoon stroll. Still, not to be completely thwarted, he went upstairs and banged the old lady over the head with a knuckled stick; he then went downstairs to get one of the table knives and cut Ada's throat whilst she was unconscious.

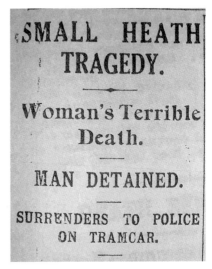

SMALL HEATH TRAGEDY.

Woman's Terrible Death.

MAN DETAINED.

SURRENDERS TO POLICE ON TRAMCAR.

John Fisher. Birmingham Gazette

Not entirely sure what to do next, he sat down and waited for Jessie to return. Luckily for her, she didn't hurry back. Fisher made himself a cup of tea and waited a bit longer. By 5.45 she still hadn't returned. Possibly feeling a little daunted by the presence of his dead partner's body upstairs, he decided to go out for a pint. He wandered from pub to pub through the evening, slowly realising what an utter idiot and madman he had been.

Jessie Dutton got back at 10.00 pm. The kitchen light was on but the door was locked. There was no answer to her knocking. She thought this was rather odd and went to borrow a key from Mrs Avern next door. With no sign of life downstairs she went up to her mother's room, possibly relieved to see her mother's shape in the bed. She pulled back the counterpane to say goodnight and discovered the full horror of Fisher's attack. Ada Taylor had suffered a vicious and ragged wound across her neck, deep enough to sever the main blood vessels. Jessie shrieked for Mrs Avern and the other neighbour, Mr Bullen. They came running but it was all too late, Ada had been dead for at least four hours. They sent for Doctor Ladell in any case. For all of the effort John Fisher spent on sharpening the knives, the doctor described the wound as being caused by a blunt instrument.

And what of Fisher? By now he had climbed on to the top deck of a tram, not really knowing where to go. A policeman, Constable Charles Brent, was just walking down the aisle of the tram. Fisher whispered into his ear: 'I have done a murder in Wright Street, I want to give myself up to you.' Constable Brent and another officer on the patrol, grabbed him by the collar and whisked him into Coventry Road police station.

At his trial on 4 December John Fisher stood little chance of being acquitted, having confessed everything. He tried to absolve himself by saying that he never meant to harm Jessie, but the judge and jury where not convinced. On 5 January John Fisher met a certain Mr William Willis, briefly. William was the state executioner.

CHAPTER 20

Edwin Thick
1930

It took some nerve to carry on exploring that gruesome cavity.

Policemen are supposed to be good at smelling a rat, but there are times when they would rather not. This rather unsavoury tale dates from 1930 when the unfortunately named Edwin Claude Thick and his wife, Ivy Emma, moved into their new Corporation house at 169 Kings Road, Kingstanding.

The two of them had been living with his parents since their marriage in 1928. No doubt they were thrilled to finally get a place of their own and on 26 August they moved in with their little baby Jean, just eighteen months old. It was the last that anyone ever saw of Ivy.

On 28 August, Edwin's parents were surprised to get a letter from him. It read:

Dear Mum and Dad,

   Ivy has gone and left me. She has gone with the Frenchman de Fray, who we met three years ago. I didn't know until she left that she has been seeing him nearly every day since. So I am sending Jean to you. Please look after her well while I look for Ivy. I have sent the new furniture back, and will get the other things. You can use them and sell them if you like. I wonder why God has been so unkind to me. I thought we were going to be so happy and I had got everything so nice. I have put as much of Jean's things as I can into the case. If I can find her I will bring her back and start all over again. Don't worry about me, mother and dad. I am alright. I feel too rotten to write anything more now. So goodbye for a bit – Your loving son Claude.

Well, what could they say? They gave the letter to a friend of theirs, Mrs Botteley, to take to Ivy's mother, Mrs Clara Brisker.

They weren't very impressed with the way Ivy had run off with a Frenchman.

Ivy's mother was as completely surprised about the strange turn of events as the Thick family. She hurried round to find out what on earth had happened. She was deeply worried. Ivy had always been a good daughter and they had seen each other at least once a month. Clara Brisker felt she would have noticed something if Ivy had been carrying on with a Frenchman behind Claude's back.

The very next day a friend of Claude's turned up carrying the baby Jean and the case of her clothes. It was back to nappy changing for the elderly couple. Mr Yates told them that Claude had asked him to bring her to them while he went shopping.

Days and then weeks passed, Claude was busy at work, little Jean was being cared for and there was no sign of Ivy at all. On 12 September Mrs Brisker was beside herself with worry and decided to go to the police and report her missing. Their response was not what she was expecting. They told her that it was Claude Thick who had to make the Missing Persons Report because he was her husband. Clara went round to the Thick's and told them that she expected him to get to get on with filing the report.

Clara Brisker received a bitter blow when she opened a letter on 15 September:

> *Dear Mr & Mrs Brisker,*
>
> *Just a line as promised on Friday. I have seen Mr Botteley and been advised not to do as you suggest, as Ivy left of her own free will, and Claude was not obliged to do anything in the matter. We have not heard anything since you were here on Friday. I have removed all the things from the house and given up the keys. I am pleased to say little Jean is keeping quite well. If you hear anything of Ivy will you let us know and I will do the same.*
>
> *Yours sincerely, A. Thick*

Mr and Mrs Brisker were obliged to wait even longer for news of their daughter. Mrs Thick had got pretty much all the household goods back from the house, with the annoying exception of the set of bedclothes. Of these there was no sign at all and Claude could offer no explanation, no matter how often she asked him about it. A bread knife seemed to have vanished as well. Things do get lost in a move so she thought no more about it.

October passed with no more news of Ivy and by mid-November Clara Brisker went back to the CID. She wasn't getting fobbed off with any excuses this time. She absolutely insisted that they do something and they opened an investigation. For a month there was little action and certainly no sightings of Ivy or the mysterious de Fray.

Eventually, in mid-December, the police decided to have a look in the house that the unlucky couple had shared for just one day. Chief Superintendent Burnett, Detective Inspector Sterry and Mr Ballard of the City Surveyor's Department searched the empty house. It looked like a pretty forlorn hope of finding anything there.

The trouble was that there was a funny smell in the bathroom and they couldn't quite work out where it was coming from. It wasn't the drains. Inspector Sterry noticed a trap in the ceiling and the other two managed to push him up into the roof space. He peered around by the light of a torch. Crawling around on top of the joists he discovered a hole in the ceiling which opened into a cavity between the wall of the house and the one next door. He shone the flashlight into the darkness.

He found himself looking at what appeared to be a blood-stained pillow and other bedding. He couldn't reach any of it, so struggled back through the small trapdoor and told the others of his find. Mr Ballard sent for one of his workman to come back with a sledgehammer.

As the bricks were smashed out of the way a large pile of bedclothes was revealed. Inspector Sterry started to move one of the bundles. As he moved it, a human hand stuck out. It took some nerve to carry on exploring that gruesome cavity. All in all they found nine bundles, each containing some part of Ivy as well as a pile of her clothes, a bread knife and a hammer. The search for Ivy Thick had ended.

The police gathered up the various bits of Ivy and took them to the coroner. He had the particularly unpleasant task of trying to find out how she had died. Despite the cool weather, there wasn't a great deal to examine.

STRUCK ON HEAD WITH HAMMER?

Husband's Alleged Statement: "I Don't Know What I Did, But—"

"GONE WITH FRENCHMAN" NOTE.

Edwin Thick. Birmingham Gazette

Detective Sterry and the Chief Inspector went around to the Thick house. They gathered Claude and his parents in the living room. Agnes Thick recognised the bread knife and hammer as those of her son. They then told them that they had knocked down the bathroom wall and discovered Ivy's body. Claude sat down and burst into tears.

'What have you done to her?' asked his stunned father.

'I must have killed her, dad. We were all right when we went to bed, but the next thing I knew was that Jean was pulling at me and then I found her dead ... You know I have some fits come over me as when they found me at Sparkhill. I don't know what I did, but I must have killed her somehow. I must have put her behind the wall. When I came to on Wednesday morning, it must have been late in the morning, when Jean woke me. I brought Jean down. I stopped with Jean. The breadman and the milkman came and I gave Jean some milk. I did not know what to do. I must have hid her then.'

'What's all the lies you have told us?' his father exploded.

'Well, dad, I had that funny feeling come over me.'

The coroner had to call in Dr Lamb of Birmingham University as well as Professor Morrison. After a rather grisly jigsaw they decided that Ivy had received at least five heavy blows to the head with a hammer that rendered her unconscious if not actually dead. There seemed to be strong possibility that her throat had then been cut, but it was difficult to sure on account of there not was really enough left of her to be sure. Professor Morrison commented: 'The dismembering of the arms and legs was not a simple operation and there were signs that the dis-articulation was not unskilfully done.'

Detective Inspector Sterry charged Claude Thick with murdering his wife by striking her on the head with a hammer on or about 28 August 1930. Claude's comment was: 'Ah, he has got it right there I think.'

Edwin Claude Thick spent the rest of his days in a secure lunatic asylum.

CHAPTER 21

Victor Betts
1931

It all seemed simple and foolproof.

There are a few common sense rules when it comes to large sums of money. The first is that if you are carrying big bags of the stuff, never follow the same route at the same time of day for years on end. Some thief is going to cotton on sooner or later, and then a robbery is almost inevitable. Another rule is that if you are going to steal said large sum of money, don't use a bright yellow car when virtually all the other ones are black, it's dumb.

Victor Edward Betts was a twenty-one-year-old blacksmith with a nasty streak. He was a big man with black hair and a very red complexion. His trade as a blacksmith gave him prodigious strength in his arms from wielding a heavy hammer all day long. He supplemented his proper income with a few robberies on the side, and he was known for his callous use of extreme violence during these robberies. Late on 22 June 1930, he went along to the garage on the Warwick Road in Greet with his friend, Frederick Lutwyche. The garage was still open and the two of them entered, browsed for a minute or two and then Betts picked up a tube of solvent and went to the till. Lutwyche handed Harold Chalmers a £1 note and as the old man opened the till Betts made his move. He smashed him over the head with his fist, knocking him clean over. As Harold Chalmers struggled back up Betts bashed him back down again, and then again. Fred Lutwyche managed to grab all the cash from the till and Betts smashed Mr Chalmers one more time before the two of them fled into the night. They had half-killed a man for a grand total of £4.

Betts kept a low profile for a while after that. However, he did have some information that might prove very profitable if he

Six Ways in Aston has changed dramatically since Victor Betts carried out his vicious robbery. Author's collection

could find the right accomplice. Every day an elderly man working for William Taylor and Sons Ltd, the drapers at Potters Hill, made a short journey on foot to the bank with the company's takings. He was as regular as clockwork and carried the cash in a leather bag on his shoulder. On 16 July he met Herbert Charles Ridley and they discussed the idea. Ridley was currently unemployed and desperate for money, and he was also a professional driver. The two of them hatched a plot to grab the loot. Ridley was to hire a car and wait for Betts to snatch the bag from the old man then the two of them could motor off at speed. It all seemed simple and foolproof. Ridley was unaware of Betts' predisposition for mindless violence.

On the morning of 21 July the two of them met up. Ridley had been to the Labour Exchange to try and get some dole. He had had no money for three weeks and his wife was giving him hell about it. They decided to rob the old man that day. Ridley went and hired a car from Young's Garage; it was a bright yellow four-seater. He drove down to Six Ways and picked up Betts. They drove around the block until they spotted the old man walking down Rifle Crescent towards Victoria Road. Ridley stopped the car not far in front him.

Sixty-three-year-old William Thomas Andrews was not expecting anything unusual on his regular trip to the National Provincial Bank at Six Ways. He walked past the bright yellow car. Suddenly, Betts leapt on him from the running board of the car and smashed him on the left side of the head with an almighty blow. The old man was instantly knocked out and dropped to the ground. Betts reached down, snatched the bag, threw it into the open back door of the car and dived in after it. Ridley gunned the engine and the car shot forward, out into Victoria Road.

Charles Dowd was in a car just coming up behind Ridley, he saw the whole attack and how the car suddenly leapt forward, rounding the corner into Victoria Road on the wrong side, with the door swinging open. He attempted to follow it, but Ridley was an experienced driver and soon vanished into the traffic. Back in Rifle Crescent William Andrews lay inert on the pavement.

Mrs Blears ran the corner shop on Victoria Road. She noticed a man lying on the pavement and hurried across to see what the matter was. He was in a sorry state, his face all bruised and cut where his glasses had been smashed into his forehead. There were signs of a blow to his left temple, too. Mrs Blears raised the alarm, managed to get another lady to fetch a policeman from point duty at Six Ways, sent some one else to Taylors to tell them what had happened and even managed to find a chair and help the old man onto it. He was dazed and concussed, clearly needing hospital treatment. Within the hour police stations all around the city were on high alert, stopping motorists in yellow cars on all the main roads out of the city.

Two hours later the alert was withdrawn, the yellow car had been found abandoned in Claverdon Street, and in a public lavatory not far away the leather bag that had contained the cash was found, empty. At first William Andrews seemed to be only mildly concussed, but as time wore on the hospital grew increasingly concerned about him. He was drifting in and out of consciousness. By the next morning he was in a critical condition. His thin, frail skull had been fractured in two places, one where Betts had dealt him a hammer like blow, not merely cracking the bone, but stoving it in like a boiled egg. The second fracture was where William had crashed to the ground, his spectacles driven into his forehead by the force of his fall. He hovered on the edge of the abyss for another day. On 24 July he died. The hunt was now on for a pair of murderers, not just a couple of thieves. The problem was that the police had no idea where to look.

There were few leads to start with, but the various times Victor Betts had waited in Rifle Crescent watching his victim had not gone unobserved, it was a small, quiet street and the presence of a stranger aroused suspicion. Nora Woodings, a young girl of just eleven, had clearly wondered what he was doing hanging around, and she gave a fairly detailed description. The garage that had hired the car to Ridley came up with a description of him. The days passed and the police started to look into their files to see if there were any similar robberies. There was at least one, the garage in Greet.

Betts and Ridley had snatched a small fortune. The bag contained £908, all in cash. The two of them had left the city by train for Portsmouth. After a couple of days there they went up to Leeds and treated themselves to a car. This cost £60. A leisurely drive down to Brighton occupied another few days and once there they set about spending their loot on watches, jewellery and girls. May Norris and Beatrice Stone were both from Bristol and thought the high life was great fun. Not without its scary moments though, on 7 August they crashed the car on the way to Southsea, but these two rich lads just got another one. It was all a great break from their usual dull work as box makers.

Ridley was uneasy though. He had seen the newspapers and their grim accounts of how William had passed away. He knew he was a hunted killer. He wasn't the only one. Betts' erstwhile accomplice, Frederick Lutwyche, was frightened he would be implicated in the murder. He decided to go to the police and admit his part in the Greet robbery whilst distancing himself from anything to do with the killing. The police were getting a more detailed picture and this was being circulated across the whole country.

Detective Sergeant Thomas Wells of Brighton Borough Police had seen the descriptions and as he was on duty on Brighton's Grand Parade, noticed someone who answered the description to a tee. He walked up to Ridley and put his hand into his pocket to check he had no gun.

BANDITS' DAYLIGHT COUP IN BIRMINGHAM.

Bank Messenger Felled and Robbed of £900.

VICTIM'S GRAVE CONDITION

A SENSATIONAL daylight robbery occurred in Aston, Birmingham, yesterday, when a bank messenger was felled by a motor bandit, and robbed of £908. The assailant was accompanied by another man in a waiting motor-car, which was immediately driven off at a high speed, and was later found abandoned.

The messenger, William Thomas Andrews, of 4, Barton's Bank, Aston, was removed to the General Hospital, where he lies in a very critical condition.

BANDITS ABANDON CAR.

Victor Betts. Birmingham Gazette

Ridley said: 'I haven't got a shooter; I am the man.'

A quick search turned up £146 in his other pockets. He admitted some of the money was from the robbery and was instantly arrested. Back at their lodgings, Betts was arrested and another £236 was found. Detective Inspector T Dillon was given the job of bringing them back to Birmingham. On the long train journey Betts told him: 'I didn't know he was dead until I saw the papers. I can't make it out as I only struck him with my fist.'

Ridley agonised during the journey, saying: 'I was surprised when I saw the amount of money in the bag. It was like a fortune to me. I should have sent some home only I thought they would think my wife was in it too.'

The two bandits came to court on 4 December. Charles Dowd had identified Betts as the man he saw strike the old man

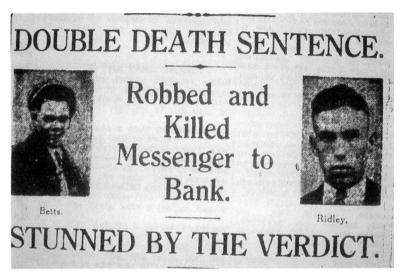

Victor Betts. Birmingham Gazette

down and snatch the money bag. The presence of so much cash in their lodgings was damning evidence too. There was a long argument as to whether Mr Andrews had been hit with a blunt instrument. When the police searched the abandoned car they found a couple of tyre levers on the floor in the back. It was an important point. Dr Gore of the General Hospital did not believe that the massive depressed fracture could have been caused simply by a blow from a bare fist. Mr G Haswell-Wilson, Professor of Pathology at Birmingham University, agreed with him. They believed that Betts had used either the tyre lever or knuckle dusters, and that meant that he had premeditated an assault of lethal force. Herbert Ridley went into the witness box and tried to defend himself from the charge of murder. He had no idea that Betts intended to strike the man and that was no part of their plan. He was, he assured the jury, just the driver.

Victor Betts was not called to give any evidence. The question for the jury was a choice between manslaughter or murder. They deliberated for an hour and came back with their verdict: both men were guilty of murder.

As the death sentence was read there was a stunned silence in the court. In the public gallery both Ridley's wife and his mother fainted in shock and had to be helped out by some police women. Ridley himself collapsed as he was led down

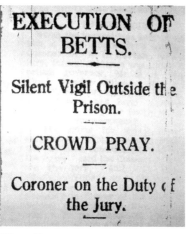

Victor Betts. Birmingham Gazette

the steps from the dock. Betts stared straight ahead, the blood draining from his normally ruddy cheeks.

The following weeks were filled with petitions and pleas to the Home Secretary to reprieve the men from the gallows. The execution was set for 3 January and the two men waited for their final doom in the confines of Winson Green Prison. As the New Year dawned, a reply came from London. Ridley was reprieved and the sentence commuted to life imprisonment. For Victor Betts there was to be no reprieve, he had struck down a frail old man with one mighty blow of his fist, completely callous to the damage he had inflicted.

On 3 January, Thomas Pierrepoint, assisted by Alfred Allen, put Victor Edward Betts on the trap inside the Dead Room of Winson Green Prison. Outside, 400–500 people attended a vigil in protest at the death sentence. As the town clocks struck 8 o'clock the crowd all removed their hats and fell silent but for one man reading a prayer. The silence lasted for ten minutes; there was no tolling of the prison bell to announce the completion of the dreaded deed. The prison gate slid open and the Under Sheriff of Warwickshire came out and pinned a notice on the gate. It simply stated that Victor Betts had undergone his sentence.

There was a growing revulsion against the death sentence across the whole country. Executions were becoming increasingly rare and attracting crowds of protestors where once they were the scene of public entertainment. Times were changing once again.

CHAPTER 22

The Revenge of Jeremiah Hanbury 1932

... her skull was battered with two heavy hammer blows and a ragged cut ripped right across her throat.

Revenge is a singularly futile affair, creating nothing but even more suffering. Unfortunately, the old saying about digging two graves before going out for revenge never seems to occur to the vengeful. In a blind fury plenty of the characters in this book have ensured their own doom whilst destroying someone else.

Jeremiah Hanbury was a puddler (furnace worker) by trade and had been the lover of Jessie Payne since 1928. James Payne was either ignorant or indifferent to his wife's infidelity. Jerry was a very frequent visitor to the Payne's house at No. 11, The Leys, Brockmoor. James was a driver and so away quite a lot of the time. Jessie and Jerry got on fine, and year succeeded year with no fuss or trouble. They were old enough to behave like adults anyway, she was thirty-nine and he was forty-nine.

The cosy relationship hit the rocks in July 1932. Jessie told Jerry to stop visiting her. Jeremiah Hanbury could not believe that this was the end of his snug, if adulterous affair. It couldn't possibly be his fault, so he came to believe it must be because Jessie was seeing a chap called Bert Eardley. If only he could get Bert out of the way then perhaps Jessie would come back to him. He told James what he thought was going on, hoping that James would get Bert to get out of their lives. It didn't quite turn out like that though. Instead of going out and thumping Bert, James asked Jessie what was going on. She told him that it was a

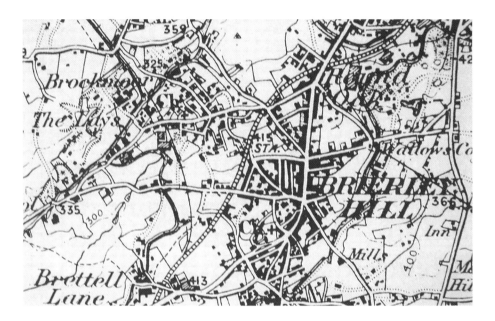

poisonous lie by Jerry and, even worse, that Jerry had raped her. James went back to Jerry and accused him of violating his wife. Jerry was having none of that and said he had paid for his sex like any other punter, and just the same as Bert was probably doing now.

Not surprisingly, they didn't have much to say to each other after that little lot. Jessie and James got on with their somewhat dysfunctional marriage as best they could. Jerry, however, was not the sort to move on from a relationship. He brooded and sulked, lashed out in a filthy temper at the slightest provocation. He lost his job and that just piled even more pressure on him. His niece, Sarah Pratt, noticed he looked wild, dark circles appearing under his eyes as he regularly sat up all night fuming about his loss. His good friend George Cullis found his behaviour really alarming. Jerry's face would writhe with conflicting emotions of rage and temper, hopelessness and anger. On 16 October, George was simply paralysed by the sheer horror of these facial contortions. Jeremiah Hanbury was slipping over the edge.

At lunchtime on 17 October, Jessie and James were in their house. Jessie had planned to go to the cinema that afternoon,

MAN'S VAIN DEFENCE OF INSANITY

"I Can't Remember Anything at All About the Crime"

JURY'S BRIEF ABSENCE

JEREMIAH HANBURY, AGED 49, AN UNEMPLOYED PUDDLER, WAS AT BIRMINGHAM ASSIZES YESTERDAY

Mrs. Payne was found dead in a pool of blood in the kitchen of her house. She had sustained two fractures of the skull and a throat wound 7½ inches long.

Those injuries, it was alleged, were

Jeremiah Hanbury. Birmingham Gazette

and come back for supper. James decided that rather than hang about an empty house he would pop out for the afternoon. He set off at 1.30 pm.

At more or less the same time Jerry Hanbury went into the *Brockmoor House* pub and had several stiff drinks. At 1.50 pm he left and made his way to No. 11, The Leys. It seems Jessie let him into the house. A few minutes after two, Edith Harris, her neighbour, saw Jessie shaking out a tablecloth in the garden. Five minutes later, Jerry Hanbury stepped out of the back door, blood pouring from a ragged wound across his throat, and spread across chest.

'Come on, I have done it now,' he muttered in a matter-of-fact voice, and lurched off out of the garden.

Edith hadn't a clue what he meant, and it didn't sound important to her. Quite what the cut and blood meant she had no idea. Given the somewhat tumultuous love life of her neighbours, she decided not to intervene. Out in the High Street Jerry was lumbering along, losing blood and muttering to himself in a low voice: 'Jerry said revenge, Jerry's had revenge.' It frightened the wits out of Mrs Louisa March. He had a wild glassy stare in his eyes. Luckily, there was a policeman nearby. PC Kirkham

An everyday object, the cut-throat razor often lived up to its name. Author's collection

found Jerry shouting at him: 'Come on, something terrible has happened. I have killed her. I am coming to give myself up.'

The policeman sent for an ambulance before Jerry bled to death, and wondered who it was Jerry had referred to. A horrified scream from The Leys gave him a pretty good idea. Frank Hill also heard the neighbours scream and raced into the kitchen of No. 11. On the floor lay Jessie; her skull was battered with two heavy hammer blows and a ragged cut ripped right across her throat. She was dead.

Jerry spent a fortnight in hospital. The wound in his throat was self-inflicted, made with a standard 'cut-throat' razor. When the police showed it to him he admitted it was his. The police had found it beside Jessie. They had also found part of a right forefinger with it, he had a corresponding wound. His hammer was still in the kitchen too. All in all the evidence was watertight. There was no way that he could deny killing Jessie. All he claimed was that he couldn't remember a thing after having a drink at *Brockmoor House*.

The trial was on 8 December. The only possible defence was that he was insane and this was a sudden, and unpremeditated attack. The prosecution pointed out that he had carried a hammer to the house, was a vengeful and jealous man with a reputation for lashing out. He wasn't mad but bad. The jury agreed. Mr Justice Humphries sentenced him to death with no qualms at all.

Jeremiah went to the gallows on 2 February 1933. Thomas Pierrepoint, the hangman, was now assisted by his son, Albert. Outside Winson Green Prison there were no significant protests against the death sentence. Most people considered Jeremiah Hanbury got exactly what he deserved. Jessie had her revenge.

Stanley Hobday and the Value of Finger Prints 1933

Gladys screamed as she saw a knife sticking out of his bloodstained back.

Most of the murders in this book have been simple to solve. It's hardly a challenge when some blood splatt-ered individual wanders up to a policeman muttering about revenge. Since nearly 90 per cent of these murders are distinctly domestic the police rarely have to look outside the household for their chief suspect. It is when there's a robbery with a related murder that their work becomes difficult.

There was a particularly nasty robbery that went horribly wrong. At 1.40 on the morning of Sunday 27 August 1933, in the house of Charles William Fox in Moor Street, West Bromwich a hideous crime occurred. Charles and his wife Gladys had gone to bed a bit after midnight. They were only in their early twenties and had got married just two years before. Around 1.30 am Gladys was woken by the sound of breaking glass. She roused Charles and he struck a match and lit the gas mantle. Someone was downstairs. Charles shrugged on his shirt and crept downstairs with Gladys just behind him. The candle he was carrying spluttered in an unusual draught. Gladys stayed on the last step as he walked towards the open window.

As Charles went to close the window a gust of wind blew out the fragile light. In the darkness Gladys suddenly heard foot-steps and a scuffle, but she could see nothing. Terrified by the grunts and oaths of the fight she retreated upstairs. Suddenly she heard Charles half-shout, half-scream 'Oh' and he started up the stairs. He staggered into the lit bedroom. Gladys shrieked as she saw a knife sticking out of his bloodstained back.

He sat down in agony, trying to reach the wicked weapon but fell off the chair. As he fell his weight drove the knife even further, right up to the hilt. He rolled under the bed in his pain and within a few minutes he had drawn his last breath.

Sergeant Gibbs of the West Bromwich Police arrived soon after Gladys raised the alarm. He found Charles was beyond help and tried to remove the knife from his back. It was lodged so hard that he had to use both hands to wrench it out. It turned out to be a sheath knife, the type used for camping trips with the back being serrated to form a saw blade. The handle was inset with a series of coloured rings. Downstairs, he discovered that the sash window had not been opened at all; someone had carefully cut away the putty and pulled the glass sheet out. Something must have gone awry because the glass was shattered on the ground beyond the window.

As daylight dawned it became clear that the burglar was probably wounded too. Some of the shards of glass had bloodstains on them, there were spots of blood on a few of the bricks in the yard and, even more interestingly, there were three footprints preserved in the soil. The police made some plaster casts of the footprints and found that they corresponded to a size 4 shoe, indicating that the burglar was a small man. The window pane that was removed was also small, so they were looking for a shorter than average crook. The police surgeon, Dr W Arnold, and the local doctor examined Charles Fox and found that he had been attacked from behind, stabbed a total of seven times before he could get back upstairs. All the wounds were in the middle of his back, confirming their suspicion that the assailant was of no great height.

It was proving to be a busy weekend for the West Bromwich police. By mid morning another burglary was reported only a few hundred yards from the Fox's house. After lunch yet another robbery was reported, at 200 Bromford Lane.

Mrs Elsie Maud Newton got up on the Sunday morning and went into the kitchen to make breakfast. At first she was puzzled by the fact that there was a needle and thread in the grill pan. She knew she had left it on the sitting room table threaded with a fine string the night before. Worried, she looked about. There was a bowl of dirty water in the sink and on the draining board was her husband's razor, with lather containing dark stubble on it. It couldn't be her husband's – he was blonde. On the table was an empty milk bottle, which should have been both full and in the cupboard. She searched further and found that £10 in cash, her gold ring and a cigarette case was also missing. The back door was unlocked. When the police arrived they had the good sense to check the bottle for finger prints and keep samples of the shavings in the bowl.

The day just kept getting busier for the police. At 1 o'clock Winifred Randle, a local school teacher, noticed that the doors of her garage were open and went to investigate. Her pride and joy, a neat little 7 hp Jowett car, was gone. She reported the theft straight away.

Detective Constable Smout was starting to get an idea of what had happened. The burglar had been disturbed by Charles Fox and after stabbing him squeezed back through the window, only to slip and cut himself on the glass outside. A short while later he had found the Newton's back door un-locked and casually pilfered the money and other items. He must have felt secure there because he had drunk a bottle of milk and taken the time to sow up what ever bit of his clothes had been cut by the glass, and also have a shave. He then checked the nearby garages and found Winifred's Jowett car and driven off in it. Just who this diminutive thief was remained to be seen. The police had a rogue's gallery of pictures and they sifted these down to a list of twenty, based on height. There was possibility of three entirely unrelated burglaries, but that seemed to stretch the imagination too much

Earlier that fateful Sunday morning, Thomas Conlon was working in the poultry yard of Manor Farm, High Legh, in Cheshire. There was the roar of a speeding car and he looked up just in time to see it somersaulting across the road. As the car embedded itself into the ditch he saw a young man wearing a dark blue coat and brown hat struggle out of the wreckage. He dragged out a map and started looking intently at it, another car passed by but didn't stop. The man set off on foot towards Knutsford.

Thomas Conlon alerted the local police to the matter, but as yet no one had any reason to connect the incident with the affair in West Bromwich. The dramatic reports in Monday's news-papers were soon to stir memories.

FINGER-PRINT EXPERT "HAS NO DOUBT"

Defence Puts Questions About Reliability of Such Tests

LONG STATEMENT READ

ONLY one witness, Mr. William James Rigby, the County Analyst, remains to be called to-day before the case for the Crown against Stanley Eric Hobday, 21-year-old West Bromwich electrician, accused of the murder of Charles William Fox, at West Bromwich, on 27 August, is concluded at Staffordshire Assizes.

One of the principal witnesses yesterday was Det.-Insp. Cherrill, the finger-print expert, of Scotland Yard. After a searching cross-examination by Sir Reginald Coventry, he told prosecuting counsel that he had no doubt that the finger-print impression found on the bottle of milk in the home of Robert Arthur Newton, of 200, Bromford-lane, which was entered by an intruder on the night of 26-27 August, and on the starting-handle of the car which disappeared from the garage of Miss W. L. Randle, and was found deserted and damaged between Knutsford and Warrington were those of Hobday.

Counsel for the Crown are Mr. W. G. Earengey, K.C., and Mr. A. Ralph Thomas, and Sir Reginald Coventry and Mr. A. J. Long are for the accused.

MISSED CAR

Petrol in It for Over 100 Miles

The first witness yesterday was a West Bromwich school teacher, Winifred L. Randle, of 141, Bromford-lane, who said she garaged a 7-h.p. Jowett car on Saturday, 26 August.

Witness added that he knew there was a man wanted by the police, and he had seen his photograph in a paper.

DID NOT OBJECT

P.C. Tells of Questions to Hobday

P.C. Elgar, of the Cumberland police, said that in response to a message from the employer of the last witness he went out in a car and in a lane leading to Rockliffe Marsh saw a man picking blackberries.

He asked the man where he came from, and the reply was "West Bromwich." When witness asked his name the man said "Hobday." Witness asked: "Is your name Stanley Eric

SUPERINTENDENT CLARKE,
one of the witnesses yesterday.

there, I thought a policeman had found it and taken it.

"I went down Newton-road, down the back of Hallam Hospital, and then made my way to Lombard-street, West Bromwich. I had a look round to see if anyone was on High street, and made my way down to Moor-street. I then went down Braybrook-street. I kept on until I came to Lyttelton-street, where I wandered about a bit."

SLEEPING OUT

Further Movements in Alleged Statement

The statement continued:
"I went down to the Gas-works and through an opening there, and I slept out until it was light. After that I started going North on the money I had got. I slept out at Burnside on Sunday night. That is between Oxenham and Windermere. Then, in the morning, I went up to Carlisle. It was raining practically all day and night, and I got soaked through. On Wednesday morning a police-officer picked me up.

"I thought they wanted me because they'd found something in my bag. I did have a sheath-knife. I bought it in the Bull Ring, Birmingham, about a fortnight ago. I gave 5s. for it. I packed it with the other things."

Dealing with the discovery of the case in the motor-car, the Superintendent said the contents included a tent, a blank-cartridge pistol, a tin of blank cartridges, and an oil stove. There was neither knife nor sheath in it. He found some keys in the car which would lock and unlock the case,

IDENTITY PARADES

In reply to Sir Reginald Coventry, witness admitted that immediately after the accused's father had left him on 31 August he told Hobday he would be put up for another identification. Hobday had already been identified by six people. It was then that he made the statement admitting being at Warstone Fields and having had a knife and a tent.

Asked what was the object in showing Hobday the suitcase on 3 September, the Superintendent replied: "He said he had lost a case. If his knife had been in it, it would have materially assisted him."

When Hobday was told that the suitcase had been found in the car at High Legh, he replied, "That's funny."

"ON PURE CHANCE"

When he showed Hobday a knife you

Fingerprint evidence was still novel enough to be seriously questioned when Hobday came to trial. Birmingham Gazette

The description of the knife was sufficiently detailed to ensure that two lads who had been camping in Warstone Fields came forward. They told the inspector of a man who had been in a tent next to theirs who had just such a knife. They were shown the photographs of all the suspects and they had no hesitation in picking out one man. Stanley Eric Hobday had been camping in the same field up until all the campers were moved off the site on Saturday 26 August.

By Tuesday morning his name and picture was circulated not only through the nation's police forces, but also in the national press. A team of detectives was sent to inspect Miss Randle's car. Inside they found a suitcase containing a tent that matched the boys' description, and a blank-cartridge pistol, a box of blank cartridges and an oil stove. They spoke to Thomas Conlon and showed him a selection of photographs, but he had been too far from the car to be sure who the individual was. The police were in better luck when they interviewed Evelyn Clarke. She had been in her mother's shop in High Legh early on Sunday morning when a suspicious looking man banged on the shop door. He bought some cigarettes and matches and went off so quickly she didn't have a chance to give him his change. She looked through the photographs and instantly picked out Hobday's picture.

The trouble was that there was no sign of Hobday at all. He had set off on foot from the car crash and could have gone in any direction. On Wednesday morning his photo was in the national papers once again.

At 7.30 that morning Walter Barber was walking along a lane outside Carlisle when he saw a man in a dark blue coat coming towards him. The man took out a handkerchief and held it over his face as he passed. Walter thought this was very odd and, thinking of the article he had just read in the paper, hurried to Rockcliffe Farm and told his boss, Mr Watt, that he thought

The beginning of forensic analysis is evident. Birmingham Gazette

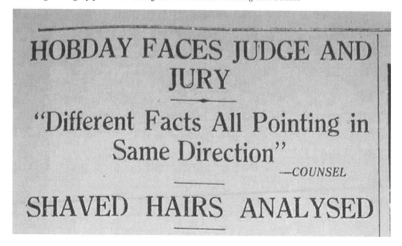

HOBDAY FACES JUDGE AND JURY

"Different Facts All Pointing in Same Direction"
—COUNSEL

SHAVED HAIRS ANALYSED

that this was the man the police were hunting. Mr Watt telephoned the local police.

PC Elgar was despatched to check the lanes around Rockcliffe Marsh. As he drove along the narrow lanes he spotted a man picking blackberries. He stopped and asked him where he was from. 'West Bromwich,' was the reply.

'Is your name Stanley Eric Hobday?' asked PC Elgar.

'Yes,' came the reply.

PC Elgar told him he was wanted for an interview and Hobday agreed to get in the car and go to the station. He was in a sorry state, tired and hungry, complaining of a wound on his left arm. He told the policeman that he had fallen off a bicycle a fortnight ago. In the station they checked his arm, there was a badly bandaged cut on his left elbow, but the local doctor didn't think that it could possibly have been caused by a fall from a bike a fortnight ago, far more likely to be a cut inflicted just a few days before.

At Carlisle police station Stanley Eric Hobday was formally charged with the murder of Charles Fox.

'Murder ... I've done no murder,' he said.

Hobday was remanded in custody, but kept denying that he had killed Charles Fox. He was brought back to Birmingham and the police started to draw their evidence together for the prosecution.

Hobday's fingerprints were found on the starting handle of the Jowett motorcar as well as on the bottle of milk left at the Newton's house. His stubble from shaving in prison was compared with the residue that was left in the house, and proved an almost identical match. The trouble was that none of this evidence proved that he was the man who stabbed Charles Fox. The footprints found in the garden were a good match to Hobday's, but the various bloodstains on his jacket could not be analysed accurately enough to determine which blood group they came from.

It was a fairly flimsy case that came to court on 14 November 1933. Stanley Hobday was charged with the murder and pleaded not guilty. He had no alibi, he admitted he was walking in the vicinity at the time in his statement. The police had tried to get him to admit the knife was his, but he wasn't that daft. One of the lads, Gilbert Pursell, who had been camping by him in the week before the murder did identify the knife positively, and it transpired that only nineteen had been made of that type, and only six had been sold in Birmingham. Sir Reginald Coventry QC led the defence and was scathing about the way the prosecution tried to conflate the stolen car and break-in near-by with the case of murder that was being tried. He had more trouble with the footprints from the garden, these were the crucial evidence that placed Hobday at the scene. There was plenty of argument about the fingerprints too; were they as unique as they were supposed to be? Jurors in Birmingham had never had to weigh up the value of this comparatively new technique in such a serious case.

Mr Justice Talbot gave a long and detailed summary of the case before the jury retired. He was very even handed about the prosecution and defence evidence. He raised some very pertinent questions such as whether the police had devalued the identity parade by showing some of the witnesses a photograph of Hobday beforehand. The jury took half an hour to reach their decision. They found Stanley Hobday guilty as charged. Mr Justice Talbot donned the black cap and pronounced the grim sentence.

During the month before his execution there were two petitions raised to the Home Secretary. One asked for the sentence to be commuted because Hobday was insane, but since there was no evidence or even argument about this matter, the petition was dismissed. The second one was based partly on the humanitarian principle that the death penalty was inherently wrong and partly that there was still some reasonable doubt that it had been Hobday that did the murder; the evidence was circumstantial. The Home Secretary was not impressed by this either. He refused to intervene.

Stanley Hobday had his appointment with Thomas Pierrepoint on 28 December 1933. Small compensation for the flood of tears that Gladys Fox shed every day through the trial.

CHAPTER 24

Eli Richards
1941

Jane's blood was all over his jacket sleeve ...

Usually, the police don't have to look that far for the murderer, but just once in a while the victim isn't the wife or girlfriend, or even a relative. This is normally when the police have a real challenge, but for this case tracking down the assailant was fairly straightforward. By now you will have got used to undiagnosed mental problems caused by head injuries, the effects of the demon drink and the usual precursors of a nasty moment in the city's history.

Eli Richards was forty-five in 1941. He had been blown up at Ypres in the First World War, receiving a nasty head wound and he had served in France in the early days of the Second World War. He was now crippled, walking with the aid of a stick. Not surprisingly, his doctors advised him not to drink alcohol on account of his head injuries. Eli worked as a labourer at the ICI Metals factory and had a reputation for getting argumentative after a few beers. He could argue the back legs off a donkey and his voice could drown out a whole pub in the process.

In the evening of 28 March 1941, he met Jane Turner in a pub. She was just as fond of the beer as he was. Jane had left her husband nearly two years before and worked as a housekeeper for John Franklin in Farmer Street since then. Her skills as a housekeeper gradually disintegrated as she descended into an alcoholic haze. By the start of March, John Franklin decided she was making more mess than she was cleaning up, and gave her notice. Her job ended on 27 March, so when she met Eli in a pub she was homeless and destitute. She was sixty-four and hardly in a state to start her life all over again.

Although the two of them had much in common, both being loud-mouthed, argumentative alcoholics; this wasn't going to be a marriage made in heaven. By 9.00 pm they staggered into *The Bell* in Bristol Street and had yet another round of drinks. Eli found a soldier to harangue and got into a particularly loud argument with him. The landlord, Percy Puddephat, put up with the row as long as he could bear and then asked one of Eli's workmates, Bert Pedley, to get him out of the pub before a fight started. Bert Pedley, Eli Richards and Jane Turner stumbled onto the No. 71 tram to head home. Bert stayed on the tram when Eli and Jane got off at Pebblemill Road. He assumed that Jane would be going to stay with Eli at his lodgings in Castle Road. It was about 11.30 pm that he last saw them.

Some ten minutes later, Robert Farman and Frank Walsingham were on their Home Guard patrol when they found the ill-matched couple arguing. They were standing in the middle of Bournville Lane, each blaming the other for getting off the tram at the wrong stop. The chances are that they had got on the wrong tram in their beer-befuddled state. They were a long way from Castle Road. The Home Guard officers listened to them argue and finally, when they asked how to get to Franklin Road, Kings Norton, pointed out the way for them to walk.

By the time the pickled pair had got to Franklin Road they were having a blazing row. They woke up half the street. Albert Vaughan heard the argument tail off into a scream, but didn't think anything very serious had occurred. What he didn't realise was that Eli Richards had smashed the end off a beer bottle and repeatedly punched it into Jane's face. The old woman couldn't possibly defend herself against this sudden frenzied attack and went down under the hail of sharp-edged blows. Eli gave up his attack after a few minutes and made his way home. Jane's blood was all over his jacket sleeve and he had dropped both his red silk handkerchief and his walking stick.

Jane lay on the cold pavement bleeding profusely and gradually losing the last of her strength and heat. The blackout was in force and no one was around to rescue her. She died sometime before half four in the morning. At 4.45 am Kenneth Hewitt tripped over her body and raised the alarm.

It didn't take the police long to work out that Eli Richards was the last person known to have seen her alive. They went to

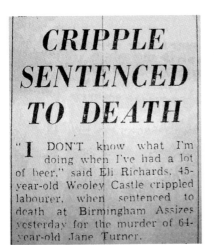

CRIPPLE SENTENCED TO DEATH

"I DON'T know what I'm doing when I've had a lot of beer," said Eli Richards, 45-year-old Weoley Castle crippled labourer, when sentenced to death at Birmingham Assizes yesterday for the murder of 64-year-old Jane Turner.

Eli Richards. Birmingham Gazette

interview him and he admitted that the stick and handkerchief were his, but told them that he had left her perfectly well in Franklin Road having given her half a crown to find some lodgings. The scratch marks on his face took a bit of explaining; he had fallen over and lost his stick was his rather flimsy excuse.

The police didn't believe a word of his story, and neither did the jury. Mr Justice Stable was not exactly enthralled with the tale either. He sentenced Eli to death on 22 July. Eli's comment on being sentenced was probably not unique: 'I don't know what I'm doing when I've had a lot of beer.'

Thomas Pierrepoint knew exactly what he was doing on 19 September, executing Eli Richards for the murder of Jane Turner.

CHAPTER 25

Harold Oswald Merry
1942

Harry dragged her body across the field ...

Sometimes a mid-life crisis can have tragic consequences. Harry Oswald Merry was a forty-year-old,
settled and stable family man with a wife and five
children, living at 205 Hewell Road, Redditch. With the out-
break of the war he started work as an aircraft inspector at
one of the factories 'somewhere in England'. By July 1941, he
became quite besotted with one of the shorthand typists in the
office.

Joyce Dixon was flattered by his attentions and soon became
just as infatuated with him. She may not have been the most
emotionally stable girl. She was now twenty-seven and it was
three years since she had had any treatment for her mental
problems. Nonetheless, the two of them flirted at work and
soon started seeing each other outside as well. Harry had managed to 'forget' to tell her about his wife and kids. They were
such an item that in January 1942 Joyce took him home to meet
her mother, Kate Dixon. Joyce was still living with her mother
at 8 Rowan Way, Northfield. Kate seemed suitably impressed
by Harry Merry and, although she was fiercely protective of her
daughter, approved of Harry's attentions.

Mrs Merry had no idea of what was going on at all. Harry and
Joyce became more deeply infatuated and, at the end of March,
Harry asked Joyce's mum if he could marry her. She said that he
could and the very next day, 21 March, the two of them went
down to London to buy a ring and other wedding items. They
spent the week at the *Museum Hotel*, Bloomsbury Street. The
manageress, Doris Webster, remembered them being a very
loving couple, quite besotted with each other.

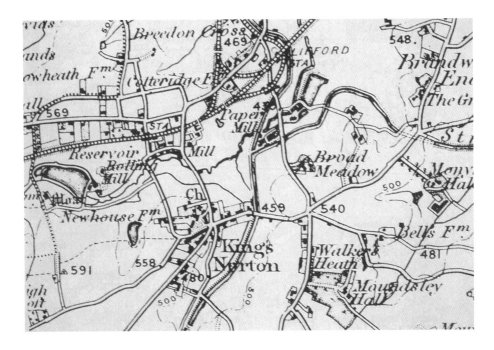

Back in Northfield, Kate Dixon discovered that Harry Oswald Merry was married and had five children. She was furious. Joyce came home on 27 March and received a shock. She had known nothing of the man's other life. Kate Dixon called him for everything and told Joyce she must give him up.

Joyce met up with Harry the next day and confronted him with the facts. Harry swore that he had always intended to tell her about his wife, but the time never seemed right. Now he said he intended to divorce her and the two of them would be free to get married then. Joyce, as besotted with him as ever, said she would stand by his side what ever may happen. When she told her mother she received such a dressing down, accused of being a little tart – and worse, so that by tea time on Sunday the 29 March she fled in tears from the house.

The couple met up later that evening at a field near the pool at Turves Green, near to Kings Norton. Joyce's already friable nerves were quite shattered by the ferocious scolding and Harry wasn't in that much better state himself – it seems that he may have had something of a row with his wife on his return from London. His affair wasn't much of a secret once Kate Dixon had discovered it. The two star-crossed lovers moped about and finally decided that if they couldn't live together, at least they could die together. Harry got out his notebook and they wrote a brief note in it:

Joyce and myself have been living together as man and wife in London, hoping I should get a divorce. So we are going to die together. Joyce knew I was married . But for God's sake forgive her. She is happy now. She knows we are going to die. So good-bye to you all. We are terribly in love with each other.

Beneath this they each signed their names. Harry took out his spare tie and pulled it tight around her neck, hoping that she would lose her nerve and beg him to stop. Quite the opposite, she pulled the noose tighter herself. In a few minutes she slumped to the ground, unconscious. Harry dragged her body across the field and pushed it into the pool. Then he sat by the water's edge and tried to strangle himself with his tie. The thing simply broke. He sat there dazed, smoked a cigarette and decided to throw himself into the water beside his lover's lifeless corpse. Splashing into the muddy shallow pool, he found it wasn't deep enough. A picture arose in his mind of his five children and a voice said to him: 'Don't do it.'

Cold, soaked to the skin and emotionally destroyed, Harry Merry walked back through the night to his home in Redditch. He got in some time before dawn and Florence stormed out of the bedroom and into the kitchen.

It wasn't long before she was answering the door to Victor Dixon, Joyce's brother. He was out looking for her since she hadn't come home that night, and hadn't turned up to work either. The two of them were probably discussing what a dreadful mess things were in, when they heard a strange noise from upstairs. He shot up the stairs two at a time and burst into the bedroom. Merry was half-hanging from the ceiling, an electric light cord wrapped tightly around his neck. Victor grabbed him and struggled to release the cable. It was so tight he could barely get his fingers under it to undo the knot.

'What have you done with my sister? You have murdered her.'

'Yes,' replied Merry, 'that's right. I will take you to her.'

Smoked by Young Woman He Murdered at Pool

HAVING given his version in the witness-box for over an hour and cross-examination of him having concluded when Mr Justice Croom-Johnson said to counsel for the prisoner: "Haven't you asked the prisoner enough?"—Harry Oswald Merry, aged 40, an aircraft inspector, of 205, Hewell-road, Redditch, was sentenced to death at Birmingham Assizes, on Saturday, for having murdered Joyce Dixon, single, aged 27, a typist, of 8, Rowan-way, Northfield, Birmingham, with whom he had had an association.

Harold Oswald Merry. Birmingham Gazette

Victor called the police straight away. Constable Joseph Porter was despatched to check the pool at Turves Green, where he duly found Joyce's body floating inert in the water. The post-mortem revealed that she had not been dead when he pushed her in, only unconscious. She had drowned.

To start with, Harry Merry admitted that he had killed her, but once he was charged with murder he retracted his confession, produced the suicide note that they had both signed, and said that after he had strangled her, he had gone away for ten minutes. On his return she had vanished, presumably dragging herself across the field and jumping into the pool herself. It was this change of story as much as anything else that swayed the jury to find him guilty of murder rather than the lesser charge of manslaughter. In a country at war there was little sympathy for a plea of insanity. There was enough death around with every single bombing raid for the antics of one emotionally weak man to warrant much attention. Harold Oswald Merry was summarily condemned to death by Mr Justice Croom-Johnson on 18 July 1942. He was hung by Thomas Pierrepoint at Winson Green on 10 September, finally re-united with his beloved Joyce in the chill of the grave.

CHAPTER 26

William Quayle
1943

The door closed with an awful finality.

There are some crimes so despicable, some characters so loathsome, that researching a book like this leads to nightmares and a profound sense of horror. Never mind all the tricks and special effects of the film industry, true horror is born in the twisted depths of a perverse mind, and it lurks a fraction of a second away from ordinary life. A couple of drunks battering each other to death is one thing, the terminal abuse of an innocent child quite another altogether.

William Quayle was a forty-nine-year-old loner who had drifted around the country after leaving his home town of Manchester. By the time he reached Birmingham in 1942, he had had countless jobs, mostly getting sacked because he drank too much. In Birmingham he managed to get a job as a works policeman on the night shift at Fisher and Ludlow's and rented 132a Bath Row. From the grimy windows he watched the school children playing in the street outside.

Vera Clarke was one of those children, only eight years old. She attended the nearby school in Piggott Street. Vera used to go home each lunchtime for a bite to eat with her mother, Ada. The 5th May 1942 was just another normal day for the family. After school Vera was supposed to go home to Essington Street and wait for her mother to get back from work at 6.30 pm.

Vera left the school with her friend, Janet Blount, but Janet went her own way home soon afterwards. Vera was trying out her new skipping rope in Bath Row at 4.45 pm when William Quayle opened his door and said something to her. Another school friend, William Abbotts, couldn't quite hear what was said, but Vera took a piece of paper from the man and ran off towards the greengrocers down the road, merrily skipping all the way. Winifred Dooling served her 3 lb of potatoes and the little girl went back towards 132a Bath Row.

It was 4.50 pm. Dorothy Binnion watched Vera take the bag of potatoes in through the door to Quayle's house. The door closed with an awful finality. Inside, she was alone. Quayle gave way to his vilest lusts, battering and abusing the child until his perverse desires were sated. As though that wasn't enough, he then took a piece of string, wrapped it around her neck and garrotted her.

William Quayle casually wandered off for a few drinks in the local pubs and phoned up work to say he was sick so couldn't go in that night. Vera's body was left sprawled on his kitchen floor.

As Quayle settled down to his beer, Ada Clarke returned home to find not a single sign of her daughter. She called up her husband, Charles, and they went around to Vera's teacher, Reginald London. He told them that Vera had left school as usual. Alarmed, the three of them started hunting around the nearby streets. Their search for Vera carried on through the evening and on into the night. By now, most of the neighbourhood was awake. They met Dorothy Binnion, who told them that she had seen Vera at Quayle's house, taking the bag of potatoes inside. The four of them set off and were soon hammering on the door.

A somewhat bleary-eyed Quayle opened the door. Charles Clarke asked where Vera was and Quayle told him that no child had come in that evening. Charles insisted that he be allowed to come in and search the cellar. Little did he realise that it was not the cellar but the kitchen that he should be searching. His daughter's body lay in there as Quayle calmly fended off his questions. Quayle said that would be fine, but just as he was about to invite them in, changed his mind saying that he had lost the key. Quayle closed the door in their faces.

They went straight to the police station and roused the officers on duty. It took a while but they got back to the house accompanied by Constable Cyril Smith. They banged on the door for a while, but it was clear Quayle had gone out. Constable Smith scouted around the house and found that he could just squeeze himself through the grating to the cellar. He got

Death Sentence on
Works Policeman

STRANGLED 8-YEAR-OLD GIRL

FOR having murdered eight-year-old Vera Clarke, of 49, Essington-street, Ladywood, Birmingham, William Quayle, aged 52, a works policeman, of 132a, Bath-row, Birmingham, was at Birmingham Assizes yesterday sentenced to death.

It was stated the girl was brutally assaulted, ravished and strangled, and later left buried under bricks in a bombed house. Quayle pleaded "Not guilty."

William Quayle. Birmingham Gazette

inside and performed a quick search before opening up the front door. It was not a moment he relished.

Constable Smith stepped out of the door holding a child's coat. Ada's heart-rending sob was as much confirmation as he needed. A closer search revealed Vera's skipping rope stuffed down the side of the armchair. Mr and Mrs Clarke went home deeply concerned and PC Smith went to raise the alarm. By the time the officers returned Quayle had returned, pretending to be a picture of innocence. He couldn't explain how Vera's coat and skipping rope had got into his house. He was asleep all afternoon, he told them. That didn't convince anyone and he was arrested and put in a cell.

By the evening of 6 May, Quayle had decided he could no longer hide the truth. He offered to take the police to the place where he had hidden her body. He took them to the back of 12 Spring Vale, where a bomb-shattered pile of bricks lay at the back of the ruined building. He told them that he had brought her body there on a hand-cart in the dead of the previous night, and covered her with bricks. The officers scrabbled with their bare hands at the rubble and found her sad remains. Quayle was charged with murder there and then.

Quayle refused to admit that he had raped the little girl despite the evidence. When the police uncovered her she was naked apart from her socks and left shoe. Her legs had been

Winson Green Prison – there were no protests about Quayle being hanged for his hideous crime. Author's collection

bound together with some brown cloth, but beneath that they found binding twine was still tightly tied around her ankles and waist, and around her neck in a lethal loop. His next statement contained the damning confession:

> *She came back into the house and something came over me. I can hardly remember, but I seemed to rush at her all at once. I must have strangled her, I suppose, and I left her lying on the rug in the kitchen. I hardly knew what I was doing. I did not interfere with her I know I done it, but I do not think I was responsible. I had a kind of brain storm.*

Mister Justice Wrottesley disagreed, he thought he was very responsible indeed and so did the jury on 12 July. The hearing was fairly brief, the defence put up a half-hearted attempt to excuse Quayle by saying he must have been mad to do it, and he was drunk at the time too. That cut no ice with anyone and he was sentenced to death.

Quayle was bullied in prison, and made several attempts to kill himself. No one was running around raising petitions to save him from the gallows. The general opinion was that this was exactly the kind of case that the death sentence should be used for. On 3 August it was carried out by Thomas Pierrepoint at Winson Green. There were a fair few people who wanted the re-introduction of public execution, not some anonymous notice pinned to the prison gates.

CHAPTER 27

James Farrell and the end of Capital Punishment 1948

He grabbed her throat and kissed her so she could not breathe ...

Capital punishment slowly fell into disuse during the twentieth century until it was finally abolished. Even in the nineteenth century it was gradually becoming viewed with distaste and in many cases there were protests and petitions. Our society became less certain of its value as a deterrent, so many murders were spur of the moment outbursts of rage that the rational process of thought required by deterrence simply wasn't involved. The perverted minds of child killers saw no further than the gratification of their lusts and took no heed of the consequences of their actions. The insane should be treated not executed. As executions now took place in private, the element of public retribution that turned the gallows into a public spectacle and warning had gone. Public opinion started to turn against execution as a suitable punishment for most criminals. The debate is not over yet and every now and then some demented nutter does something so foul that most people agree that death is probably too good for them. The debate can get very heated and complicated and this book is not a suitable forum. Suffice it to say, the last execution in Birmingham took place in 1949 with a vociferous public protest against capital punishment.

James Farrell was an eighteen-year-old who really hated his army service. Not surprisingly, he ran away from the barracks and, with nowhere else to go, returned home to his family in Bevis Grove, Kingstanding. The trouble was that army service was compulsory and sooner or later he would have to return. It was a prospect that preyed on his mind. On 20 November 1948, his father, Nathaniel, came downstairs into the kitchen to find James lying on the floor with his head by the oven, the gas taps wide open. James was semi-conscious but not dead. There was so little credit in the gas meter that the gas supply had shut off. Whether this was a deliberate attempt to commit suicide or a frantic plea for help remains as mystery. It certainly shows that James was in a bit of an emotionally delicate state.

The next day, his family gave him a bit of cash and told him to go to the cinema to cheer himself up. He went to the Odeon at Perry Bar. It was in the cinema that he met Joan Marney. They chatted away for a while, watched a film and chatted some more on the way out. Joan told him that she was seventeen-and-a-half, and responded passionately to a kiss or two. They decided it would be fun to sneak into Sutton Park and have a bit of fun in the bushes. Once inside the Banner Gate entrance, they snuggled up near a holly bush and started kissing in earnest. James was getting very excited.

The one thing that Joan hadn't told James was that she was really only fourteen and should be home by 9.30 or her mum would be furious. She told James that she must go home. James was furious and pushed her onto her back, pulling at her clothes, intending to finish what he had started. Joan protested even louder and told him she would tell the police.

James was already in enough trouble for being absent without leave, frustrated by his lack of success with Joan and now facing an accusation of attempted rape, something snapped inside. He grabbed her throat and kissed her until she couldn't breathe, then throttled the life out of her. Once her feeble struggles subsided, he got up and walked quietly home.

Joan's body was discovered early the next morning. Police enquiries soon found plenty of people who had seen the two of them at the cinema and they had a good description of her assailant. James Farrell was unaware of this when he decided to hand himself into the police as an absent without leave soldier, presumably hoping that he would be sent directly back to his barracks and thus a long way from the scene of the crime. He walked into Steelhouse Lane police station.

The officers at the station immediately saw that he matched the description of the murderer that they were looking for. They

Strangler executed

JAMES FARRELL, 19-year-
old Army absentee, of 4,
Bevis-grove, Kingstanding, Bir-
mingham, was executed at
Winson Green prison yester-
day for the murder of Joan
Marney (14), of Sidcup-road,
Kingstanding.
  Farrell strangled the girl in
Sutton Park last November.

James Farrell. Birmingham Gazette

got him into a cell and questioned him. Farrell offered no resistance and admitted the charge, giving the officers a detailed statement of exactly what had happened. He was stunned to discover that Joan was only fourteen.

James Farrell was held in custody until his trial on 10 March 1949. His defence was to be one of insanity; his mother was in Lodge Road asylum, he had attempted suicide the day before the murder, and the murder itself was an act of madness. Despite the months available for the defence to mount a thorough case on his behalf, when the trial commenced Mr Vaughan brought forward no witnesses at all. Indeed, he described Farrell's act a 'shocking crime' which was the work of some 'frenzied man'. He went on to describe Farrell's attitude as 'so callous and indifferent' that he could not have known right from wrong. With a defence like this it is hardly surprising that Mr Justice Lynskey started his summing up: 'You may well think that this man must be a monster.'

The jury had little trouble finding James Farrell guilty of wilful murder. In the couple of weeks that he was in the condemned cell he passed his nineteenth birthday and on 29 March he was led to the gallows.

On the due date a crowd of over 100 people gathered outside the gates of Winson Green. There were prayers read and flowers thrown and even tears shed for the confused young man who became the last person executed in the grim confines of Winson Green Prison.

Select Bibliography

Old & New Birmingham, Robert K Dent, Houghton & Hammond, Birmingham, 1880.

A History of Birmingham, Chris Upton, Phillimore, Chichester, 1993.

The Making of Victorian Birmingham, Victor Skip, Birmingham, 1983.

Haunted Birmingham, A Smith & R Bannister, Tempus Publishing, Stroud, 2006.

One Morning in May, Patrick Hayes, Brewin Books, Studley, 2002.

Aris's Birmingham Gazette, 1817.

Warwickshire Advertiser, 1817.

Index

People

Places